Puerto Rico 1898:
The War After the War

Puerto Rico 1898: The War After the War

FERNANDO PICÓ

Translated from the Spanish by
Sylvia Korwek and Psique Arana Guzmán

 Markus Wiener Publishers
Princeton

For information write to:
Markus Wiener Publishers
231 Nassau Street
Princeton, NJ 08542
www.markuswiener.com

Library of Congress Cataloging-in-Publication Data

Picó, Fernando.
    [1898. English]
    Puerto Rico, 1898 : the war after the war / Fernando Picó ;
translated from the Spanish by Sylvia Korwek and Psique Arana Guzmán.
    Includes bibliographical references.
    ISBN 1-55876-326-0 (alk. : HC)
    ISBN 1-55876-327-9 (alk. : PB)
    1. Puerto Rico—History—1898-1952. 2. Spanish-American War,
1898—Social aspects. 3. Outlaws—Puerto Rico—History—20th century.
4. Peasant uprisings--Puerto Rico--History—20th century. 5. Puerto
Rico—Economic conditions. 6. Puerto Rico—Social conditions. I. Title.
    F1975.P47 2004
    972.95'04--dc22
                                    2003055934

Printed in the United States of America on acid-free paper

Table of Contents

Preface to the Edition in English

In the last fifteen years historians in Puerto Rico have researched, discussed, and written extensively about the Spanish-American-Cuban War of 1898 and its consequences for Puerto Rico. Much of the ongoing discussion has run along predictable lines, but some interesting new avenues of research were opened on the occasion of the 1898 invasion's centennial. Right before the centennial, Carmelo Rosario Natal edited an extensive bibliography, *El 1898 puertorriqueño en la historiografía,* which attempted to arrange published works within the framework of ongoing discussions. Lanny Thompson published *Nuestra isla y su gente: La construcción del 'otro' puertorriqueño en Our Islands and Their People,* in which he analyzed the visual representations of Puerto Rico circulated after the war.

For the centennial of the war the Association of Puerto Rican Historians edited two books. One, *Los arcos de la memoria: El '98 de los pueblos puertorriqueños,* revolved around the municipal events accompanying the change of command from the Spanish to the American government. The variety of circumstances and experiences showed not only the social and political differences of 1898 but also the plurality of current historians' viewpoints. The second book, *Cien Años de Sociedad: Los 98 del Gran Caribe,* assembled papers presented at the Association's 1998 congress and showed the wider Caribbean context of the war and the invasion. The Ponce Museum of Art edited *'98 Cien Años Después,* a collection of papers presented in early 1999 by a wide array of scholars.

Another commemorative congress resulted in the publication of *1898: Enfoques y perspectives,* which added the Spanish and North American perspectives to the war. In Madrid, Consuelo Naranjo and Carlos Serrano edited the papers from another congress. In *Imagenes e imaginarios nacionales en el ultramar español* several Puerto Rican papers were included, which dealt with the invasion and its aftermath. Other publications, before and after the centennial, highlighted the importance of the commemoration in Puerto Rico of the war that changed the political destiny of the island.

What all these publications had in common was the desire to shift the emphasis from the military events of the war to the social, economic and diplomatic elements which the war dramatized. Instead of the few actors of the traditional historiography, the new studies highlighted the roles assumed and played by the many. The search in judicial, municipal, diplomatic, and journalistic sources enriched the offerings of the military archives. The cataloguing and microfilming in the 1980s and the 1990s of thousands of Puerto Rican newspapers made it possible to follow the vicissitudes of the American occupation in the major towns. It also made evident the many divisions and conflicts existing in Puerto Rican society at the end of the 19th century.

This book examined one aspect of the social conflicts of the time. When it came out not everyone welcomed the examination of the old social woes and divisions. In the early decades of the 20th century to forget past divisions had become the norm, and traditional historiography had unwittingly passed over the grave events that developed after the war had ended. Even pointing out that the fabled outlaw, *Aguila Blanca*, had been in New York when the invasion took place shook some devotees of his myth. But once the dust of controversies settled, the *partidas* became a stable element of the considerations around 1898. Although much more has to be done to understand the social cleavages of 1898–99, younger scholars doing dissertations and exploring the judicial archives have taken up the unending task of understanding the war and its aftermath.

Preface

"The most visible people in the town of Dorado," according to the newspaper *La Correspondencia de Puerto Rico* in its August 8, 1898, issue, "are in the habit of gathering in front of the house of the parish priest—an excellent gentleman, by the way—for the purpose of exchanging impressions about the burning issue of the day. While gathered there a few nights ago, a passerby directed their attention to a beautiful, luminous point that sparkled in the sky, believing it was the Yankees' balloon. Immediately, spyglasses of various powers were trained upon the object in question, and in the end, all were convinced that it was nothing other than the planet Venus." That was the end of that evening's gathering. There were four days of combat still to come, but that was the only instance after the July 25th invasion and before the armistice that the press in the capital paid any attention to the fate of Dorado during the war.

Cabo Rojo, on the other hand, did not accept being bypassed by the military operations. In a session of the town council on August 14, 1898, the mayor, Manuel Montalvo Colberg, declared:

> . . . as is well known, the troops of the United States Army, while marching from the city of San Germán to Mayagüez on the tenth of this month, had perforce to travel across the jurisdiction of this municipality, where they engaged the Spanish troops in a brief skirmish, which did not hinder the Army's progress towards Mayagüez; and since that department is under the occupation and military domination of the American troops, Cabo Rojo being part of that department, in fact and legally Cabo Rojo is also under their control; and of course it therefore follows that this municipality and the areas under its jurisdiction be declared to belong to the United States of America.

The town council then declared that Cabo Rojo belonged to "the above-mentioned American nation." The mayor hoisted the flag of the United States from the balcony "to the cheers of 'Long live American Puerto Rico! Long live the United States of America! Long live Cabo Rojo!'" Later, the mayor informed General Schwann of this self-proclaimed annexation.[1]

It is interesting to re-encounter the effervescence, the rumors, and the expectations manifested in Puerto Rico during the summer of '98. "There are those who say our country will be called 'Richland.' That name shall soon be, under the American administration, richly deserved." That appeared in *La Correspondencia* of the 20th of August. But two days later, "a letter from St. Thomas claims that the Americans have signed up 15,000 individuals of the colored race to come and settle in Puerto Rico, offering them advantages that no one would disdain."

However, while the well-to-do segments of society were busy specu-lating about the future, buying English grammars and deliberating about changing the names of the streets, the farm workers and small landown-ers in the countryside were settling accounts with the past. To understand fully what 1898 meant to Puerto Ricans one has to look beyond the epigrams of the elegant journalists of the day and beyond the solemn deliberations of town councils.

In 1898, the United States invaded a Puerto Rico that was seriously divided by social conflicts. The violent nature of the American interven-tion in the country also gave rise to violent expression of those pre-exist-ing social conflicts.

This view of the immediate impact wrought by the invasion on the lives of Puerto Ricans runs counter to two quite different and naive images of the year 1898 in Puerto Rico. One of these visions is shared by those who assume that Puerto Rico, before the invasion, was peaceful, prosperous and united. The other is favored by those who believe that backwardness, intolerance and opression reigned before "the arrival of the Americans."

Both images of Puerto Rico previous to the Spanish-American War tend to promote moralizing interpretations of our collective past. But, a history of good guys and bad, of victims and saviors, does little justice to the need of every Puerto Rican to understand 1898.

At the end of the nineteenth century, Puerto Rico was in a stage of transition towards agrarian capitalism. The sugar industry had suffered a crisis at the end of the 1870s and was still trying to recapture its former share of foreign markets. This is why the dominant elements of the sugar industry had become so acutely conscious of the island's lack of political power. They were searching for a way to consolidate the manufacturing phase of sugar production in centralized sugar mills. The high cost of mechanization, however, as well as the stagnation in sugar prices, lengthened the crisis in the sugar industry. From the beginning of the 1890s, this crisis had had repercussions on labor-management relations. Through a series of strikes the workers had demanded higher salaries in order to face the escalating cost of living, brought about by Spain's tariff policies.

In the face of pressures such as these, many sugar-cane growers preferred to convert their land to pasture. This option, of course, further complicated the situation for the sugar-cane workers, as they were displaced by cattle farming.

But if Puerto Rican sugar faced serious problems, worsened by its uncertain access to the American market, the situation appeared to be more promising in the coffee-growing zone. Coffee production in the mountain ranges of Puerto Rico had been increasing by leaps and bounds since the 1870s, stimulated by the favorable prices that prevailed in foreign markets. Fertile and inexpensive land, new access roads to the interior, the relatively simple machinery in use then, and, above all, the enormously abundant, low-cost labor supply stimulated investment in coffee plantations.

The thriving coffee-growing centers in turn served as an incentive for the development of complementary activities in the mountain districts. Artisans and laborers from the coastal regions streamed towards the coffee-growing zones to take advantage of the boom.

This boom, though, had been due to the good prices commanded by Puerto Rican coffee in the European and Cuban markets until the middle of the 1890s. Toward the end of the decade, however, it became evident that Puerto Rican coffee would gradually be overtaken by its competitors and fall prey to a drop in prices in some recently-won markets. This was due to coffee production on a massive scale in other Atlantic regions. In order to meet this challenge, Puerto Rican coffee growers needed to increase both the quality and yield of their product, which called for even greater access to credit. Toward 1898, many coffee growers were very deeply in debt to the commercial firms that had lent them capital at high interest to build the coffee mills where the grain was processed, or to extend existing plantations.

Coffee production was widely distributed among plantations of all sizes. Market conditions, however, were beginning to point toward the advantage of concentrating the processing of the beans in those units that were equipped with the most efficient, fastest means of production. Though the large farms were not dominant in total volume of production, they were in the processing and marketing of coffee. The numerous small growers obtained credit from the hacienda owners' store and then settled their debts in coffee berries, that is, in unshelled coffee beans. It is not surprising, therefore, that the relationship between larger and smaller producers led to conflicts of interest.

Bringing coffee from the mountains

Sugar and coffee dominated, but did not monopolize, the economy of Puerto Rico in the 1890s. Cattle farming, tobacco, subsistence crops and the cultivation of cash crops rounded out agricultural production. Although manufacturing played a very small part in the economy, the production of cigars and cigarettes in small and medium-sized shops and the numerous artisans' shops in the towns provided a living for many families. Other activities, such as fishing, salt production, and construction, rounded out the picture. It was clear, nevertheless, that these were not enough to meet the people's need for gainful employment. Both sugar cane and coffee employed a maximum of people during the height of their harvest seasons, but, save for a few exceptions, they did not offer year-round employment. Tobacco crops were harvested in small lots and for this reason workers were needed to process the leaves only a few months per year. The government encouraged the construction of public works, particularly roads, during the months of reduced agricultural activity, but those projects often depended on the meager financing that the municipalities could provide.

The precarious financial situation of the workers often was evident in conflicts that the state sought to minimize. Strikes were forbidden by law. Employers could dismiss workers arbitrarily. This state of affairs was particularly acute in the coffee-growing zone, where workers often lived in houses built by the coffee grower. To be dismissed from a farm meant also to lose the roof over the family's head.

The incipient labor movement enjoyed greater strength among workers such as typesetters, whose numbers and capabilities were enough to stop production. In rural areas, collective efforts to improve conditions tended to take on the characteristics of uncoordinated protests. As often as not these were directed against the police, rather than the employers. The fact that the government chose to downplay the importance of these manifestations of unrest, and the lack of coordination and scant organization of these activities created an image—which even the most liberal newspapers favored—that the farm workers, the *jíbaros*, were incapable of fighting for their rights.

But in 1898–99 it was impossible to underrate the joint acts of small landowners and farmworkers. This is a book about the armed bands, the groups of *tiznados*—so called because they blackened their faces with charcoal—or seditious parties which, in the months immediately after the American invasion of Puerto Rico in 1898, attacked first the farms and rural stores belonging to Spaniards, and later on those of native-born Puerto Ricans of European descent, or *criollos*.

Acknowledgements

The study is based upon the correspondence of the American military forces during 1898–99, on the records of those tried by military commissions for their participation in the armed bands, on the briefs of criminal complaints filed by the landowners who were the target of raids in the areas of Utuado, Adjuntas, Lares, Ciales and Arecibo, on documents filed in the old municipal archives of Utuado and Ponce, and on newspapers and other publications of the time.

The research was carried out at the General Archives of Puerto Rico, the National Archives in Washington, the Ponce Municipal Archives, the Puerto Rican Collections of the University of Puerto Rico in Río Piedras and Sacred Heart University in Santurce, and in the library of Northwestern University in Evanston.

This effort to approach our past with new questions is not isolated. From page one onwards, this book owes much to the historiographical discussions generated by many of my colleagues who are engaged in similar projects: Gervasio García, Andrés Ramos-Mattei, Blanca Silvestrini, Francisco Scarano, María de los Angeles Castro, Angel Quintero-Rivera, Juan José Baldrich, Arcadio Díaz-Quiñones, Rubén Dávila, Jorge Rodríguez-Beruff, Guillermo Baralt, Mariano Negrón, Rafael Ramírez, Lolita Luque, María Barceló-Miller, Carmen Raffucci, Francisco Moscoso, José Curet, Manuel Maza, Laird Bergad, Astrid Cubano, Pedro San Miguel, Lydia Milagros González, Luis Agrait, Carlos Buitrago, Sylvia Alvarez, Julio Damiani, Kenneth Lugo, Juan González-Mendoza, Carlos Casanova, Luis Figueroa, Luis Ferrao, Peter Katsilis-Morales, Luis Martínez-Fernández, Arturo Bird, Carlos Pabón, Roberto Alejandro, Israel Cardona, Félix Matos, Emilio Kouri, Pedro Juan Hernández, Gloria Tapia, Arnaldo Licier, Gilberto Aponte, Carlos Rosado, Ricardo Otero, Juan Otero, Carmen Campos, Carlos Rodríguez-Villanueva, Gregorio

Villegas, Rafael Cabrera, Ramonita Vega, César Solá, Libia González, Ramón Corrada, Jaime Pérez and Humberto García, among others.

Eduardo León, Luis de la Rosa, José Flores, Milagros Pepín and Gustavo Santiago-Rivera of the General Archives of Puerto Rico always encourage, advise, and aid me in each research project. My thanks to these colleagues! Nelly Vázquez, of the Historical Research Center, has always extended her effective help. All who labor at the Puerto Rican Collection of the José M. Lázaro General Library of the University of Puerto Rico have always given my projects sympathetic and sensitive cooperation. Very special thanks to Dr. Luisa Vigo for her efforts as coordinator of the Puerto Rico Newspaper Project, whose preliminary inventory I have found to be a valuable tool. I am indebted to Mrs. Josefina Marxuach de Rodríguez for her warm welcome to the Puerto Rican Collection at Sacred Heart University. I am equally thankful for all the courtesies extended me by the director and staff of the Ponce Municipal Archives, the secretaries of the Utuado Municipal Archives and Mrs. Annie Guiven of the Río Piedras Parochial Archives.

The University of Puerto Rico granted me a sabbatical in 1985–86 to carry out the research on which this book is based. I am particularly grateful to former Dean John Larkin, to Enrique Lugo Silva, then Director of the History Department and to the Personnel Committees of the College of Humanities and the Department of History for their confidence in me. I must also state my thanks to the Institutional Fund for Research of the Office of the Dean of Academic Affairs, which over the course of two years provided the funds I requested to carry out the classification and inventory of the collection of old documents at the General Archives, which came originally from the archives of the Superior Courts of Arecibo, Aguadilla and Guayama. Gilberto Aponte, Arnaldo Licier, Gregorio Villegas and Arturo Bird-Carmona, who were at the time studying for their Master's degrees in History, worked on this last project.

Carmín Rivera-Izcoa, Fernando Rodríguez and Mary Jo Smith of Ediciones Huracán, my publishers, have been decisive in the progress of this book. Their dedication and care are visible on each page of every book that Huracán publishes.

My Jesuit brothers, particularly Orlando Torres, Maximino Rodríguez, Francisco Morales, Confesor Ramos, José Rubén Colón, Jorge Ambert and Jorge Ferrer encouraged me during the writing phase. And the Jesuit community of Caimito, Puerto Rico, would not be fully represented here if I did not thank Mr. Gilberto Alemán for all his kindnesses and great patience.

I am indebted also to my mother, Matilde Bauermeister, my brothers and sisters, aunts and uncles, nieces and nephews for their affection and their support.

To dedicate a book is a special way of expressing thanks and admiration. I wish I could write as many books as there are people whom I esteem. Those who have picked passion fruit and hiked up and down the hillsides of Las Planadas in Cayey with me do not need elaborate explanations to understand why I dedicate this book to my uncle and aunt, Jorge Bauermeister and Laura Nieves. And for those who have not yet done so, a couple of lines would not be enough.

Glossary

Spanish words not translated in the text

agregados   service tenants living on an estate

almudes   measure of volume equal to 20 liters; half of a fanega

componte   device for torture used in 1887 by the Spanish Civil Guard on the people who fought or conspired to overthrow the colonial regime

criollo   one born in Spanish America but of European, usually Spanish, ancestry

cuerda   land measure equal to .97 acres

fanegas   measurement of coffee volume approximately equal to 100 pounds

jíbaro   person living in the mountains, used to refer to landowners and landless alike

Muñocista   follower of Luis Muñoz Rivera, leader of the Autonomist Party

peso   an old silver coin of Spain and Spanish America equal to eight reales *quintal*   hundredweight

real   a former silver coin of Spain and Spanish America,
                   one eighth (.125) of a peso

tiznados   members of the band, thus called because they
                   blackened their faces with charcoal

CHAPTER ONE

Rural Order in Puerto Rico in the 1890s

What was Puerto Rico like before the American invasion of 1898? In the twentieth century, this question, which sounds so natural, has been fraught with emotional connotations.

In view of the impact of the economic depression of the 1930s and the evident failure of the single-crop sugar economy, some of the country's thinkers have looked back upon events in the past—before the time of the invasion—in search of a way out of the quagmire in which Puerto Rico found itself. The desire to return to a previous age, one that did not bear the mark of an economy based upon large, machine-powered sugar mills, induced some thinkers to theorize about an idyllic past: a flourishing country, not yet trampled upon by invaders, a country which produced a large variety of foodstuffs on small farms and bustling with the endeavor of thousands of independent artisans. Pedro Albizu-Campos, for example, put it this way:

> The Yankee invasion found our people spread along fertile valleys in villages founded in healthful locations, and well organized to render religious, social and public services. . .
>
> When the Yankees forced their way into our ports, we enjoyed an educational system designed to forge a strong, forward-looking community. The sexes were educated separately, boys had male teachers and girls female teachers. . . Puerto Rico was the healthiest country in the Americas. . .
>
> Puerto Rico was rich in name and fact; our Christian heritage had created a model family and a solid society; the nation appeared in the

1

forefront of modern civilization. . .

    In his reply Mr. Albizu-Campos explained that at the time of the
American invasion, Puerto Rico was a creditor nation, that the
Government of Puerto Rico and all the municipal governments had a
surplus of gold in their coffers, that wealth was fairly distributed, that
the poor of Puerto Rico were people who owned eight or ten acres of
land and had two or three hundred pesos stored up in their wives'
stockings. . .[1]

In that happy land there was no hunger, no social conflict, no overwhelming crime. . . and autonomy, the highest aspiration of the majority
of Puerto Ricans, was about to be obtained, through negotiations with the
government in Madrid.

That idyllic view of Puerto Rico in the 1890s has crumbled under the
relentless scrutiny of such researchers as Gervasio García, Andrés Ramos-
Mattei, Angel Quintero-Rivera, Laird Bergad, Guillermo Baralt, Lydia
Milagros González, Carlos Buitrago, Luis Díaz and María Barceló-
Miller.[2] In the light of these findings, it is obvious that by 1898 both the
living and working conditions of a great number of Puerto Ricans had
undergone substantial modification, through processes such as the con-
centration of landholdings into sugar cane latifundia, the mechanization
of the industrial phase of sugar production, the enlargement of cigar- and
cigarette-producing workshops and the control of the harvesting, processing, selection and shipping of coffee beans. The economic and political
structures of the time tended to favor the aspirations and interests of certain sectors, especially of the merchant class. Widespread dissatisfaction
with the social order and the virulent nature of the social conflicts induced
the authorities to employ mechanisms of repression and intimidation
which, in any case, never managed to quell resistance.

The Economic Bases of Rural Order in the 1890s

In the 1890s Puerto Rico was an eminently agrarian country. Nearly
eighty-five percent of the population lived outside of towns of over two
thousand inhabitants.[3] But the basic resource of agricultural production—

land—was not equitably distributed. In the most fertile areas of the coastal lowlands, the tendency had been for land ownership to become concentrated in large estates.[4] In the coffee-growing highlands of the Cordillera Central, small farms were numerous, but there were also large haciendas that encompassed almost all of the acreage in the *barrios*, or municipal subdivisions, such as Río Prieto in Yauco, Guilarte in Adjuntas and Jayuya Arriba, then part of Utuado.[5] Municipalities such as Camuy and Corozal, where small properties were the rule, played a complementary role in their regional economies, which did not always guarantee solvency and adequate living conditions for small farmers.[6]

Agrarian production was not oriented to the country's need for food but to the stimulus of foreign markets. By the 1880s, Puerto Rico did not produce enough to feed itself.[7] Flour, corn, potatoes, herring, codfish, dried beef, salt pork, rice and many kinds of sausages and canned foods were imported from Spain and the United States. Agronomists who wrote in the 1880s and 1890s in Puerto Rico pleaded for a more appropriate balance of production that would fulfill the basic needs of the country better and would not be as vulnerable to the price fluctuations of international markets. The appeal of rising coffee prices and the weight of investments in sugar cane production were, however, more convincing than the warnings of agronomists. In municipalities such as Utuado, subsistence crops lost ground to coffee, even though the population had doubled since mid-century.[8]

The majority of Puerto Ricans had no land of their own. In the coffee-growing highlands, the "landless" lived as *agregados* or service tenants on the farms. The owner would allow them to build huts with boards cut from highland palms, thatched with palm leaves, or else made tin-roofed houses or rooms in sheds available. Heads of families labored during the year for what were often token wages: at the turn of the century, 35 to 50 centavos of the local peso.[9] They took staples on credit from the hacienda store and paid with their labor. The debt was rarely satisfied. Only at coffee harvest time, when the whole tenant family participated, did they earn a higher income. That was when, as a rule, they purchased a change of clothes and the few utensils that equipped their households.

Wages tended to be better in the cane-growing zone than in the mountains, but only during harvest time, which at the most extended over a
period of six months. The workers lived in the lands that bordered the
towns and coastal villages, and during the off-season between harvests
tried to make ends meet by engaging in complementary activities such
as fishing, the burning of charcoal, public works projects and personal
services.[10]

Although in theory most Puerto Ricans worked for wages, it was common practice both in the lowlands and in the mountains to take staples on
credit and then settle the account with services rendered by the wage
earner and the rest of his family. The granting of credit allowed the owners to have a pool of workers to draw from as needed during cultivation
and harvest times. Until accounts were settled with a previous employer,
debtors could not work elsewhere, or move to another municipality without due permission from the municipal authorities. The hacienda stores'
account books carefully registered the workers' weekly debts and the
partial payments they made with wages earned.[11]

Small farmers were caught in a debt cycle analogous to the workers'
situation.[12] They used their harvests to settle the debts incurred during the
year, but oftentimes they still owed sums to the store owners in town
or to neighboring farmers. Sometimes they worked for their neighbors
during harvests to supplement their income. To cultivate their own land,
however, they depended on the labor of the whole family. The tendency
was for several generations to live together on those small farms, and, as
a result of close family ties, this pattern was reinforced by marriages
between cousins. Even though small properties were vulnerable due to
the economic difficulties of their owners, and to divisions among heirs,
they usually remained stable, if not in the hands of the same families then
within the same group of small-scale farmers. Ownership changed, but
the small farms were not easily absorbed by the large properties unless
the neighboring hacienda owner was particularly interested in that parcel
of land. This coexistence is understandable if we bear in mind that the
small farmer generally handed his harvest over to the hacienda owner in
payment for the debts accumulated at the hacienda store, and served as an

occasional or supplementary hired hand for harvest chores.

The financial position of medium and large farms was always precarious. Even though the hacienda owners kept their workers tied down through their debts, they in turn depended on the credit extended them by the merchants. The latter set the value of the harvests that the farmers turned over to them as debt payments, and also set the interest rates—which could fluctuate between 12 and 18 percent per year—until the final settlement was made. In this way, in doing business with farmers the merchants had three different sources of income: they set the price of the articles they sold to the farmers, they set the interest rate on the credit granted, and they determined the value of the crops they received in payment. The lack of banks, a need which was finally met in the very decade of the 1890s,[13] assured economic domination by the merchants, particularly in the highland municipalities.

The long chain of debtors did not end with the merchants, however. They in turn often purchased shipments of merchandise on credit from North American and Western European exporting firms. At this level also debts were settled with the shipment of harvested crops. And at this point the precarious situation of Puerto Rican agriculture became very obvious, because the prices paid for sugar and coffee, the two most important items in Puerto Rico's export commerce, were set not on the island but abroad.

In the 1880s the price paid for Puerto Rican sugar on its main market, the United States, remained unchanged at 2.9 cents per pound.[14] But even the scant earnings that this price allowed Puerto Rican exporters were threatened during the 1890s as a result of tariff battles between the United States and Spain.[15] In the case of coffee, prices fluctuated in the mid-1880s. Then, from 1887 to 1896, there was a memorable increase in price.[16] The best-informed people in Puerto Rico were aware that the price rise of the 1890s would not last forever, because it was due to setbacks affecting Brazilian production. The difficulties faced by Brazilian coffee growers were the incentive that was encouraging other planters in Latin America and Africa. As a result, new production would soon flood the European market, the most important one for premium-quality Puerto Rican coffee.

Loading ships with coffee

Credit and marketing problems were not the only impediments to the development of single-crop farming in the coastal lowlands and the highlands of Puerto Rico. Hauling and transportation problems also complicated matters for coffee growers. Towards the 1890s, the island's largest coffee-producing centers were located in the most recently populated zones. The great coffee plantations had been developed in inexpensive, virgin highlands. Particularly outstanding were the plantations in the most isolated *barrios* of Utuado (especially Jayuya), Las Marías, Maricao, Lares, Yauco, Adjuntas, Ciales, San Sebastián and Juana Díaz (Villalba). Communications between the coffee-growing zone and the coast, however, were poor. As a rule, the municipalities of the interior depended upon just one or two roads for access to ports that were allowed to engage in foreign trade. Apart from these routes, the *barrios* were connected to the towns by means of trails. During the rainy season, travel on these paths became very difficult and load-carrying almost impossible. The farms that did not have enough animals of their own had to hire mule trains and pay mule drivers, whose skills commanded the sort of wages paid other specialized workers. Sometimes the owners of large farms provided these services for pay.[17] The roads were unsafe, not only because of frequent rains and flash floods, but also due to holdups and a whole variety of mishaps. The outcry for new roads produced numerous projects, but very little construction. Apart from the Central Highway, few roads were considered adequate and safe.

The highway from Cayey to Guayama, a project that dated from the 1850s, was finally completed in the 1890s. Other roads, planned from the time Governor Fernando de Norzagaray was in office (1852–55), were still in the design, consultation or initial stages. The road from Comerío to Bayamón, for example, had seen only two kilometers of construction in the 30 years that plans and drawings had been sent back and forth to obtain Madrid's approval.[18]

On the coast, where sugar cane and cattle farming were located, the infrastructure was better than in the hinterlands. The main ports were connected by daily schooner service, as well as by other small vessels. By 1898, the train service that was supposed to circle the island had reached from Camuy to San Juan, from Ponce to Yauco, from Mayagüez to Aguadilla and from Río Piedras to Carolina.[19] The coastal towns were connected by highways that, in general, were considered adequate.

The island's main artery, however, was the highway from San Juan to Ponce, by way of Río Piedras, Caguas, Cayey, Aibonito, Coamo and Juana Díaz.[20] This Central Highway, which was wide, with gradual elevations and easy curves, solidly-built culverts and bridges and ditches that received constant maintenance from a system of road crews, made the crossing of the mountain range quite comfortable. Bundles of tobacco sent to the workshops in San Juan, Caguas and Cayey, mule trains transporting coffee down to the port of Ponce, loads of plantains and tubers, casks of molasses, and cattle destined for the slaughterhouses all flowed along this highway, which also saw the comings and goings of sales representatives, government officials, the mails, vendors, soldiers and volunteers sent to relieve detachments perpetually guarding the beaches, and itinerant workers in their never-ending hustle and bustle in search of a way to make a living. Ever since it was conceived as the main means of communication between San Juan and Ponce, this Central Highway fulfilled its double mission of facilitating the flow of merchandise and services between the two coasts while guaranteeing the capital's control over that area of the island which was politically and commercially most fully developed. For this reason, the Central Highway would become, in 1898, one of the principal military objectives of the United States Army.[21]

Living Conditions

The precarious condition of Puerto Rico's agrarian economy in the 1890s was fully reflected in the living conditions of the masses. In the towns, where there were doctors, hospitals and pharmacies, public health had made notable progress, but the vast majority of the rural population depended upon the services of *curanderos*, or healers, who with their traditional herbal medicine had been able to provide for a wide range of ailments and illnesses in the preceding centuries. By the end of the 19th century, however, the development of single-crop agriculture brought with it the dispossession of the *jíbaros*. As a result, the daily diet became

Cooking dinner, near Aguada

poorer, and contagious and other diseases, such as tuberculosis, anemia, bilharzia, typhoid fever and malaria proliferated. Folk medicine, with its teas, infusions, emetics, massages and poultices, could not cope with the endemic diseases from which the emaciated population was suffering.

The greatest degree of deterioration in the quality of life of the workers occurred in the coffee-growing areas, which had been rapidly populated in the last decades of the 19th century. For example, mortality rates toward the end of the century reveal a desperate struggle for life in the district of Utuado.

TABLE 1.1
Mortality rates in Utuado for selected years, between 1779 and 1899

Year	Mortality rate per thousand inhabitants
1779	8.6
1788	14.0
1802	18.0
1828	17.9
1835	17.5
1841	15.1
1856	25.6
1866	21.9
1876	29.6
1887	31.7
1899	53.5

Sources: Death registers of San Miguel Parish, Utuado, Demographic Registry, and population censuses at the Scarano Collection of the General Archives and documentary sources.

The number of deaths in the crisis year of 1899—the year of hurricane San Ciriaco—is exceptional, but it illustrates how vulnerable the population was to the famines and epidemics that followed this disaster. The excessive dependence of coffee-growing municipalities on the price that their harvests obtained abroad also kept the inhabitants hostage to the international price variations of this commodity. When the price of coffee began to fluctuate considerably in 1897, the insecurity of the highland population could only increase.

To sum up, the living conditions of the masses in the highlands of Puerto Rico towards the end of the 19th century were marked by the scourge of epidemic and endemic diseases, the harshness of plantation work, the decline in quality of the standard diet, and the economic insecurity caused by conditions in the production of coffee.

Façade of Law and Order in the 1890s

This worsening of living conditions in the countryside gave rise to acts of protest that were not always recognized as such by the press in Puerto Rico. It was necessary to preserve a façade of law and order to obtain credit in the United States and Europe. This became doubly necessary when the Cuban War of Independence broke out in 1895. Thus in its October 23, 1895, issue, the newspaper *La Correspondencia* posed the rhetorical question, *"Cui Prodest (A Quién Aprovecha?)"*:

> We have been informed by a trustworthy source that it is not just one letter (published in yesterday's paper) but several letters that businesses in this capital have received, from Europe and the United States, denying or limiting credit to firms that heretofore could be quite sure of obtaining it. The reason for this lack of confidence, as the letters themselves indicate, *is the current state of turmoil in this country*, as judged by the news being published in some newspapers.
> . . . If we should lose the credit that we have striven so hard to protect, the financial survival of an essentially agricultural and commercial province such as ours would become absolutely impossible.[22]

At aproximately the same time, an issue of the newspaper *La Democracia* blamed diehard Spanish loyalists for "making up stories about separatist movements on this island which run counter to tradition, to history, and to the very nature of this country." The writer of the editorial was in agreement with his counterpart at *La Correspondencia* about the negative effect that rumors of insurrection had upon foreign credit. He quoted a letter from a foreign business firm to a Puerto Rican one in which it was stated that

> while the present circumstances prevail, as described by some Puerto Rican newspapers, not only is it not desirable to broaden our dealings with those countries by opening new accounts but, we shall be forced to restrict our existing business dealings.[23]

In this manner, the autonomist press stifled, or tried to stifle, the rumors of struggles for independence on the island, and persisted in creating an illusion of order and serenity. However, when a journalist such as Evaristo Izcoa-Díaz, editor of *La Bomba*, tried to discuss the country's deep unrest and lashed out at government officials, he was swiftly deprived of his freedom to warn others that such boldness would not be tolerated.[24] Yet it was not conspiracies of a separatist nature that best illustrated the degree of resistance among the peasants and farm workers and the level of dissatisfaction with working and living conditions that prevailed on the island. In the final decade of the 19th century, the Puerto Rican labor movement was beginning to be a force to be reckoned with.[25] Among typesetters, construction laborers, tobacco workers and people employed in the sugar-processing factories, associations were being founded, with the express purpose of redressing injustices, to the discomfiture of management, whether pro-Spain or autonomist. These cracks in the social edifice, built upon the weak foundations of a single-crop economy, could not be so easily disguised as the political aspirations of those who sought independence.

During the 1890s, a series of strikes and public demonstrations revealed the importance and strength of the workers in the towns.

Legislation then in force, however, that made strikes illegal and allowed employers to settle many issues arbitrarily, still inhibited displays of this new-found strength. For example, on April 27, 1892, José Rodríguez-Fuentes closed his cigar factory, *Las Dos Antillas*. He gave his reasons for the firing of one hundred workers in the following release, which was published in the newpaper *La Correspondencia*:

> It is true, and I am very sorry, that the industry is going through this temporary crisis because I have lost control of the ship, and when the crew imposes its will upon the captain, the vessel starts to take on water and it's every man for himself; as for me, after forty-two years in these parts, with a terrific struggle I have made it safely through, and my children's daily bread is assured.
>
> I cannot fight against such ingratitude without giving my mind some rest in order to take up the struggle once again, for if in five days I have cast out of my house seven thieves whom I had taught to work—following the parable of Jesus which says "by the sweat of thy brow thou shalt earn thy daily bread"—and if there is no respect for the man who gives it and teaches how to earn it, then that is reason enough to postpone for a time the reconstitution of *Las Dos Antillas*.
>
> God save me! For if I had sense enough to found this business, and by dint of hard work raise it to its present position—irrespective of the best Havana has to offer in its class and development in the art of cigar production—I cannot be blamed if the workers do not measure up to the demands of the job and poverty rears its ugly head. . .[26]

Workers did not enjoy the same access to the national press of Puerto Rico as their employers. Slowly, as they warmed to the battle, they found the strength to demand redress publicly and consistently, and as they made converts to the cause of organized labor, they began to publish their own newspapers and pamphlets. In this manner, literate workers in cities and towns started permanent organizations to obtain their basic rights.

Rural Order in the 1890s

In the countryside, however, where most of the workers lived, there were fewer possibilities of creating lasting instruments to defend the workers' interests. Still, it would be naïve to assume that these difficulties in establishing the means for collective struggle totally prevented shows of opposition.

Delgado-Passapera has reviewed the cases against farmworkers who were arrested in Utuado in 1891 and in Arroyo in 1895 for acts that were classified as subversive or related to the boycotts against Spanish businesses in 1887.[27] The interesting fact about both groups of persons tried is that neither seems to have had ties to political groups from the dominant sectors of society. Most of those arrested had no direct, provable ties to Puerto Rican national political organizations. They appear to have belonged to local organizations designed to resist the economic domination of peninsular Spaniards.

On a much more spontaneous level there were many cases, recorded at the time in the Puerto Rican press and in court proceedings, of individual acts of protest. For example, according to *El Buscapié*, the following incident took place in Toa Alta on September 24, 1895:

> . . .emboldened by drink, a farm worker was making crude and inappropriate remarks about a roast pig—a sow—that a group of volunteer soldiers was going to eat after finishing their target practice. The unit commander sent the laborer to jail with two of the volunteers, who were armed. It is said that once on the road a neighbor by the name of Francisco Martínez intercepted them and requested that they let the man go free, since he had acted under the influence of drink.
> . . .The fact is that a shot rang out and Martínez was killed and the man under arrest, Plácido Beltrán, was wounded. He did not die because the bullet hit the blade of a knife he carried inside his shirt.[28]

In this type of incident, stories of personal animosities tended to become mixed up with the participants' notions of political order. In particular the *Guardia Civil*—the Civil Guard, or Spanish state police—

intimidated people, provoked conflicts and on some occasions, armed confrontations. The fine line that separated incidents related to public order from incidents related to the native-born population's rejection of the Spaniards became quite blurred, especially in the minds of the common people.

Beyond these clashes with the authorities, there were numerous incidents of gang robbery, assault and murder in the countryside. The frequency of these crimes proves how precariously the authorities held power in the rural areas, and the high level of violence that social struggles had reached by then. This is why, in the 1890s, in documentation related to hacienda owners and rural merchants, there is copious reference to shotguns, mastiffs, fences, enclosures, padlocks, locks, bolts, strong hinges, and even private telephones to link country and town.[29] And this is also why so much stress falls on administrators, stewards, bosses, overseers and superintendents, who bridge the enormous gaps that were developing between the powerful and their peons. *La Charca*, written by Manuel Zeno-Gandía, paints a vivid picture of that world of animosity, distrust and human suffering that characterized the coffee-growing highlands during the boom times. The bloodiness of the attacks carried out by seditious parties during 1898–99 is not surprising to anyone who has read or examined criminal court documents of the previous decade.

The countryside was not immune to negative influences from abroad. In November 1895, *El Buscapié* reported the discovery of "a secret society in Juana Díaz for the promotion of the deadly vice of morphine consumption," in which minors were given injections. Presumably, elsewhere on the island there were other centers that catered to morphine addicts.[30]

In these and other circumstances the state demonstrated that it had insufficient control over the territory it sought to continue governing.

Two Mentalities:
The Harmless Jíbaro and the Dangerous Jíbaro

If the State barely managed to govern the countryside, it is not surprising that each of the dominant classes tried to explain this deficiency in ways that were consistent with their political sympathies. For certain sectors closest to the Spanish regime, disorder in the countryside was evidence of the natives' inability to govern themselves: the *jíbaro*, of mixed race, illiterate, superstitious and indolent, erratic, taciturn and given to unexpected violence, needed to be compelled, once and for all, to accept the discipline of salaried labor. What the countryside needed was more policing and supervision. Only thus would the necessary order prevail on the island.[31] It goes without saying that many who were unconditionally committed to Spanish rule shared this line of thinking.

The attitude of the *criollo* sectors that favored autonomy was much more patronizing. The *jíbaro* was ignorant, but educable. His crimes were a reflection of his abject poverty. He was illiterate, and thus incapable of acts of political subversion. Basically harmless, a *jíbaro* would threaten the life of another person only when in the grips of desperation. [32] More a slave of his ignorance than a master of his fate, the anemic *jíbaro* was the dead weight that slowed the country's progress. This interpretation of the life of mountain folk did not attribute to them either political initiative or social conscience.

The year 1898 would reveal a *jíbaro* that was far different from the stereotypes developed by the dominant classes in San Juan and Ponce. For a period of time, the rural order that heretofore had been guaranteed by the owners of large plantations, but subjected to their arbitrariness and disruptions, would lack the backing of the police power that had flowed from the cities. Puerto Rico was to discover to what degree country folk had their own views about the social order.

CHAPTER TWO

The Invaders
and the Invaded

The year 1898 began with a very long drought. By mid-May, *El País* lamented: "No matter how you look at it, the weather is getting worse. It has not rained at all: February, March and April, and now May, so far, have only brought a searing sun, together with strong south winds that scorch the grasses and are even harder on the crops than the sun."[1] It finally rained during the last ten days of May. From Ponce the news was: "It has rained a great deal in this area, so agricultural activities are on the rise." From Utuado it was reported that "We have been favored with rains lately, farmers are delighted and minor crops are being planted." Shortly after, the news from Arecibo was that "farmers are happy because the heavens have taken pity on them."[2]

And rain it did. By July, the amount of rain was beginning to cause alarm. In San Juan, *La Unión* complained:

> The weather is still too wet: it has rained off and on for three days and three nights. Last night and this morning there have been long, heavy downpours. At 8 o'clock, the torrent of water that ran down Tanca and other streets in the southern section of San Juan towards the Spanish Gate was so strong that it eroded the soil and poured into the Ubarri streetcar station, flooding the station coffee shop. And it seems that the storm will continue.[3]

A month later, it was the Americans who were complaining about the rain. Carl Sandburg, a private in the 6th Illinois Volunteer Regiment, would recall in his old age the incessant rain that had bogged down the march and made sleeping difficult during his campaign days in Puerto Rico:

> We had set up our pup tents, laid our ponchos and blankets on the ground, and gone to sleep in a slow drizzle of rain. About three o'clock in the morning a heavy downpour of rain kept coming. We were on a slope and the downhill water soaked our blankets. We got out of our tents, wrung our blankets as dry as we could and threw them with ponchos over our shoulders. Then a thousand men stood around waiting for daylight hoping the rain would let down.[4]

First the rain was an adversary and then an accomplice in General Schwann's military operations in western Puerto Rico.[5] No sooner was the armistice declared than both Americans and Spaniards, within their respective territories, had to turn their attention to problems of rivers overflowing their banks, impassable roads, and illnesses related to the floodwaters. In its August 20 issue, *La Correspondencia de Puerto Rico* quoted an unidentified local daily:

> Due to this season's abundant rains, the predominant sickness is malaria; there have also been a number of cases of influenza, fortunately in its benign form. Gastrointestinal diseases have become more widespread in the last few days, with cases tending toward glandular congestion of the digestive system. There are also neuroses of all types and manifestations, all of them emotional responses to the circumstances.[6]

If not the neuroses, at least the rains seemed to paralyze the country. On October 10, *El País* stated that "because of the excessive rains of the last few days, the train tracks near Manatí have been displaced by the water. Until yesterday, train service to Arecibo had not resumed."[7] So between downpours the American military forces occupied Puerto Rico and their Spanish counterparts bid adieu to the island.

The War: From April to July

When the Spanish-American War broke out, Puerto Rico was just beginning to enjoy home rule under its Charter of Autonomy. Puerto Rican newspapers had in fact been paying more attention to the political changes related to the new constitution than to events leading to the declaration of war between Spain and the United States. Only the economic pressures generated by the imminent war forced journalists to turn their attention to what was happening beyond the mouth of San Juan Bay. A correspondent from Vega Baja had the following to say in the April 17 issue of the Mayagüez newspaper *La Bruja*:

> The election period has come and gone, and our town has returned to its monotonous lifestyle, and I say monotonous, because it is completely *dead*.
> Agriculture is paralyzed.
> Thousands of people are jobless.
> Businesses have retrenched, and the price of staples is sky-high.
> Hunger is already knocking at our doors, and the only voice heeding its call is want.
> Heaven help this country![8]

The Spanish government harbored no illusions about what could be expected should Puerto Rico become a theater of war. The island, however, was overflowing with patriotic prose. *La Bruja,* in Mayagüez, complained in May that with the war "a swarm of bad poets has invaded even the darkest corners of this country. Would-be bards spring up everywhere, singing the praises of the war, of Spain, of May 2nd, and of their old man's saber." By way of proof, it quoted a few verses that had appeared in *La Correspondencia*, which started like this:

> Arrived at last the longed-for day
> Courageous sons of noble Spain
> Yankee daring ye shall abate
> Which has provoked your rightful rage.[9]

With the inflated verse, rumors proliferated about battles, bombings, fleet movements, secret pacts, world wars:

> My uncle knows, always from official sources, where the warships are; what they lack, what they have too much of, what their admirals' intentions are, what exercises they carry out, what they will do next . . . Ships have been sighted behind Desecheo Island? He knows which ones they are. Has a lady clad in black gone to City Hall and spoken with the Mayor? He knows the reason for her call, and how that meeting is related to the conflict with the Yanks.[10]

The offers to fight to defend Spanish nationality to the last drop of blood were truly impressive. On the 25th of April, *El País* reported that San Juan "presents a delightful military aspect. . . every patriotic young person has turned into a resolute soldier; ladies from all classes have become members of the Red Cross. . . and in this atmosphere, our young ladies go to normal school to take their exams, and children go to school happily, eager to be commended for their dedication."[11]

Virgilio Ramos-Vélez, of Manatí, went to San Juan "to offer his services, those of his sons and of two hundred available men, representing that town's pro-Spanish committee."[12] A Local Defense Committee was organized in Utuado:

> We have had the immense satisfaction of seeing this town pulling together. . . forming one solid mass, all minds thinking as one, and all hearts beating in unison, full of enthusiasm because of the love they profess for the unvanquished Spanish nation, our true motherland. Of all the great and important gatherings that have taken place in this town to discuss the present circumstances and to take the necessary steps to defend the integrity of the territory and the area, the greatest and most important gathering turned out to be the one that took place last night. . . the people, cheerful and enthusiastic, responded to the patriotic exhortations of its orators. . . All the inhabitants of the city at the center of the island have signed up as soldiers with the Local Defense Committee, formed under the leadership of the lawyer *Señor* Casalduc, to defend the interests of the upstanding Spanish citizens of Utuado in general.[13]

The Church of San José in San Juan, showing marks of American gunnery

Admiral Sampson's bombardment of San Juan toward the middle of May barely interrupted this collective excitement. Many people seemed convinced that the cannonfire from El Morro had inflicted severe losses, such as the destruction of Sampson's best battleship, and that hundreds of his men had died. . . but it was obvious that Sampson's blockade had a stranglehold on the country. A lack of basic commodities—which the single-crop economy had turned into imported goods—was soon to be felt. The municipalities began to regulate the sale of such basic foodstuffs as tubers and plantains, which now became the focus of an attention they had not received in a long time. Hunger and dissatisfaction started to proliferate in the countryside.

Getting Ready for the Invasion

In May, when steps were being taken in Washington to prepare for the invasion of "Number Two"—the military high command's preferred euphemism for Puerto Rico—justifying the projected invasion was the last thing on their minds. On May 9, Philip Hanna, United States Consul in Puerto Rico, now working out of St. Thomas, informed the State Department in Washington that there were only some 4,600 regular soldiers in Puerto Rico: 2,000 in San Juan, 1,000 in Ponce, 1,000 in Mayagüez and about 600 distributed among the rest of the municipalities. There were also about 7,000 volunteers. Hanna continued:

> I am still of the opinion that Puerto Rico should be taken and held as a coaling station, thus supplying our Navy and cutting off Spain. In order to accomplish this we should land in Puerto Rico not less than 10,000 men. Let them land at Ponce or Fajardo, or some other port, and march through the Island to meet the American fleet at San Juan. Let the fleet knock down the fortifications there which are the only ones on the Island, and our land forces of 10,000 can hold the island forever. . . From Ponce to San Juan there is the finest road in the whole West Indies, and an army could march across to San Juan with no bad roads to interfere.[14]

Henry Whitney, a lieutenant attached to the newly-created Military Intelligence Service, visited the island in May posing as a British seaman, to observe the condition of the forces that the government of Spain could rely upon in Puerto Rico.[15] Upon his return on June 9, he reported that the regular troops amounted to about 8,000, mostly deployed for the defense of San Juan, that there were some 12,000 auxiliary troops, but that everywhere on the island it was strongly doubted that when the time came, the island-born volunteers would back the Spaniards in battle.[16]

Whitney noticed that it was likely that armed groups of Puerto Ricans would support efforts to eject the Spanish from the island, and he pointed out the advantages of various points around the island as possible initial bases of operation.

Major General Nelson A. Miles, 59, was nominally commanding general of the United States Army. Born into a family of smallholders in Massachusetts, Miles had become a soldier during the Civil War. At age 22 he had recruited his own company of volunteers, but the Governor, instead of naming him captain, had given him the rank of lieutenant, placing a political protegé in command. Infuriated by this injustice, the young Miles arranged a transfer to another company. Due to this painful experience, Miles would always be wary of politicians and of military officers who had obtained their commissions through patronage.[17] In the midst of the invasion of Puerto Rico, he brought about the resignation of the colonel and other officers of the 6th Massachusetts Volunteer Regiment for irresponsibility in one of the battles following debarkation in Guánica.[18] In telegrams sent at the time to the Governor of Massachusetts, the rancor of that incident in his youth was still palpable.

At the end of the Civil War, Miles held the rank of brigadier general of volunteers. He decided to remain in the Regular Army with the rank of colonel during the years following the war. He married one of the daughters of Judge Sherman, of Ohio, one of whose brothers was General Sherman and another the Republican politician John Sherman. The latter eventually became a senator from Ohio and the first Secretary of State in President McKinley's administration.[19] His family connections did not prevent his promotions from being few and far between while he remained in the West fighting Indians and avoiding a desk job in Washington. Under President Cleveland, Miles finally attained the highest possible rank for a career officer in those days, that of Commanding General of the U. S. Army. Miles had been expected to be influential during McKinley's presidency, since his wife's uncle was Secretary of State, but Secretary Sherman had to resign when he disagreed with the interventionist turn that McKinley's policy towards Cuba was taking.[20] Miles was no longer part of the inner circle of advisers to the President. As a result, he had very little influence over the military policies that the United States adopted in its war against Spain. His standing was further complicated by the outbreak of the Spanish-American War, which brought to the fore not only the generational struggle that was taking place in the Army between those officers who remained from the Civil War and the new cadres trained in the Military Academy, but also the institutional struggles between the Army and the Navy.

Miles was put in charge of the preparations for the Cuban expedition, but he soon found himself trapped between the insistent directives of President McKinley, on the one hand, who wanted a quick solution to the war before the November congressional elections, and cumbersome procedures needed to requisition and transport war matériel, to train volunteer troops, and to organize a comprehensive military plan, on the other.[21] The difficulties came to appear insurmountable. Trains arrived in Tampa crammed with boxes whose contents were not labeled. Tens of thousands of volunteers from eastern cities, who had never in their lives held a rifle or slept in open fields, complained to their congressmen and journalists about everything. Their protests ran the gamut from the bite of southern mosquitoes to the taste (and very soon, the stench) of canned meat. Worse problems were soon felt, such as the proliferation of typhoid fever, the intervention of politicians in decisions pertaining to internal military organization, and the breakdown of discipline among volunteer troops.[22]

On the 6th of June, the former consul of the United States in Puerto Rico, Hanna, sent the Secretary of State a telegram from Saint Thomas. He urged that the expeditionary forces to be sent to Puerto Rico consist of no less than 25,000 men. Hanna feared that the government would underestimate the number of Spanish forces in Puerto Rico. Miles for his part aspired to command personally an expedition made up of between 15,000 and 30,000 men to conquer and occupy "Number Two." The American press, however, speculated that the expedition would be commanded by General John A. Brooke.[23]

Once the expedition set sail for Santiago de Cuba on June 12, Miles turned his attention to the plans for the invasion of Puerto Rico. The difficulties that the American forces encountered in Cuba were duly taken into account: Miles did not want a reprise of the errors committed in Oriente Province, which had so captured the attention of the press. It was imperative that the troops undertake the campaign well equipped, with sufficient support from navy transports, artillery, the siege train for the eventual capture of San Juan, and medical personnel and equipment.

One point that turned out to be crucial to Miles' planning was the health of the members of the invading force. A repetition of the many casualties that yellow fever had caused in Cuba could not be allowed.

Since it was not yet known that the illness was transmitted by a mosquito, Miles took all conceivable precautions so his men would not carry the infection with them to Puerto Rico.[24]

When it became obvious that the city of Santiago was going to fall, Miles took an important decision for the development of the Puerto Rico campaign. In view of the fact that so many regular troops in the Cuban expedition were suffering the ravages of yellow fever, he decided to take no men who had participated in the Oriente Province campaign. That is, he would use fresh troops—but this meant that most of the expeditionary force would be made up of volunteers. The majority of the regular troops were either in Cuba, on the way to the Philippines or Hawaii, or else stationed at the various bases in the United States that were considered vital to the security of the nation.

The use of volunteers for the Puerto Rico campaign was politically expedient for President McKinley and the Republicans in power. Fed by the yellow press, the popularity of the war generated demands for citizen participation in the triumphs that were expected. All available information on the number of Spanish troops on the island coincided in that these were not sufficient to resist the projected American invasion. The blockade, destruction and capture of the Spanish fleet in Santiago de Cuba made it impossible for Spain to send last-minute reinforcements. It was expected that Spain would sue for peace as soon as Santiago fell, thus avoiding the loss of Puerto Rico and the Philippines, since the separation of Cuba seemed inevitable. Therefore, a military campaign in Puerto Rico promised to be a short and easy one, exactly what was needed to fulfill the state regiments' expectation of participation and glory. The young volunteers, who had grown up hearing tales of glory from the Civil War, were eager for the chance to emulate their veteran fathers. The war was coming to an end, however, and most of them had not seen active service. In order to appease the politicians from the northern states—whose support was considered crucial in the Congressional campaign of 1898—the Administration was trying to provide an opportunity for the volunteers from those states to prove their mettle and so get the satisfaction they desired.[25]

The use of predominantly inexperienced, volunteer troops in the Puerto Rico campaign, however, carried its risks. Many of the soldiers who had signed up for adventure in the war had scant military training. How they would react in actual combat remained to be seen. A high number of casualties among the volunteers would undoubtedly lead to political complications for Congress in an election year. Miles would have to rely more on the quantity than on the quality of his troops, and on his military hardware. It was imperative, therefore, to avoid direct confrontation with the Spanish forces. The idea was to make the enemy yield ground, to overwhelm them by the sheer force of numbers in the flanking operations. In the early years of the Civil War, encirclement had been one of the customary deployment tactics for inexperienced northern troops, when faced with veteran Confederate soldiers. The commanding general's expertise would be very useful.

Miles had agreed with Secretary of War Alger and with Admiral Sampson, who was in command of the naval forces in the Caribbean, that the United States troops would debark in Fajardo. From there, covered by the fleet's cannon power, the troops would march west to lay siege to and take the capital. When San Juan had fallen, the rest of the island would be occupied.[26]

Once on the high seas, Miles changed his plan and decided to invade through Guánica. San Juan, instead of being the first objective, would be the last. Several interpretations have been given to this decision, and it is quite likely that Miles carefully weighed most of the reasons that have been suggested for his change of mind. The one he would eventually present most vigorously, however, does not seem convincing. He alleged that knowledge of the projected landing in Fajardo had become widespread in Washington and that the Spanish were aware of the plan. For weeks, however, the press had been debating the possible landing sites in Puerto Rico, and had been insistently mentioning some point on the south coast near Ponce, together with the Fajardo option. On the very eve of the invasion, *The New York Times* indicated on the front page that the chosen site was Guánica. The surprise value in selecting Guánica was quite relative.

Perhaps the choice that Miles made had more to do with the rivalry

Spanish troops at Guanica

between the Army and the Navy. Up to that moment, the greatest glories of the war belonged to the Navy. The victories obtained by Dewey in Manila and Schley at the Bay of Santiago, as well as Sampson's maneuvers in Cuban and Puerto Rican waters, had captured the attention of the press. To march to San Juan under the protection of the Navy, would, therefore, not contribute to the prestige of the Army or its commander. In any case, the intervention of the warships' guns would be necessary to destroy San Juan's waterfront fortifications.[27]

On the other hand, an invasion through Guánica would have the advantage of delaying an encounter between Spanish and American troops, which would allow the untested volunteers to develop some confidence in their fighting ability. An added advantage of the south coast was that it would make it possible to achieve the occupation of the most populous municipality on the island—Ponce—as well as the occupation of the most vital centers of economic activity, in a relatively short time. It was known that the zone was not well defended. On the south coast, it was to be expected that, in municipalities such as Yauco, there would be support from *criollos* who were known to be averse to the Spanish regime.[28]

We could speculate, within the context of the events that in fact took place in Cuba and the Philippines, that Miles was aware of the political advantages that the United States would derive from occupying all the seats of municipal power that the Spaniards vacated. As a first military objective, a protracted siege of San Juan would have resulted in bands of island-born civilians dislodging the Spanish authorities and taking over the towns farthest from the capital. The eventual transition from a provisional *criollo* government to a military one would have been more difficult.

That, of course, is to think the historically unthinkable: What would have happened if. . .? Miles decided to attack through Guánica and the events that followed proved that he chose the most appropriate option for the annexationist interests of the United States.

The Invasion

On the morning of July 25, the ship "Gloucester," a privately-owned vessel that had been converted to military use, sent a broadside of grape-shot over the peaceful settlement of Guánica. A launch was then lowered and 30 men were taken ashore. After taking down the Spanish flag from the Customs house, and exchanging fire with the few volunteers who were defending the vicinity of the port, they erected a barricade of barbed wire at the end of the only street in Guánica.[29]

Then, following Miles' plans step by step, the invading units—the 6th Massachusetts and 6th Illinois Regiments—went ashore, drove out the scant armed resistance that they encountered and quartered themselves to wait for military supplies to be brought ashore. The night of July 26, a few nervous soldiers, alarmed because a horse had entered their camp, woke up practically the entire contingent, including General Miles, with gunfire.[30]

Even if the invasion had its farcical moments, it did not deviate from the rigidly precise course that Miles had set. On July 27, Yauco was occupied without difficulty. The invaders intalled a new mayor, who welcomed them with a proclamation that the editorial writer for *The New York Times* was to call comical for its marked obsequiousness.[31] The son of the late president Hayes hoisted the American flag over City Hall.

The invading forces traveled from Guánica to Ponce by sea. It was in Ponce that the fate of the war in Puerto Rico was sealed. From a strictly military point of view, the Spanish high command could have sacrificed Ponce to retard the advance of the invading troops and deny the United States the enormous advantage that the infrastructure of the port and the city had to offer. Destroying Ponce, however, to slow down the progress of the invasion by seven or ten days would have amounted to an invitation to general insurrection in that city and throughout the island. The innumerable appeals to the authorities from civic and consular leaders won out and the city escaped becoming a battleground. The Spanish forces retreated in a hasty but orderly manner, by the Central Highway. The Spanish had taken the crucial decision of the war: the greatest battle, unless the armistice that everyone expected occurred first, would take place on the slopes of the Asomante.[32]

Neither the Americans nor the *criollos* were hoping for decisive battles. On July 30, the mayor of Guayama sent a three-person delegation with a message for the officer in command of the United States forces in Ponce, General Wilson, saying that the garrison of one hundred Spanish soldiers had departed the city at dawn, but it was feared they would return to set it afire. Could the American forces protect Guayama? Wilson communicated with Miles in writing about this matter, and Adjutant General Gilmore made this notation in pencil on the letter: "Seen by General Miles. Will be attended to in a few days. July 31/98 J.C.G."[33]

The occupation of Guayama was an intriguing possibility, because it opened the way to advance towards Cayey, in which case the Spanish defense of the Asomante would become academic. As soon as General Brooke arrived in Puerto Rico with the troops he had been assigned, Miles put into practice this change in his plan to proceed by way of the Central Highway. On August 1, the "Gloucester" repeated in Arroyo the landing operation first tried out in Guánica.[34] Two of the ships that carried the horses, artillery and telegraph equipment, however, ran aground in Ponce and Guánica. The delay allowed the Spaniards to entrench their troops between Cayey and Guayama, in the heights of Guamaní. Even so,

Puerto Rican Commissioners accompanying General Miles's army

Brooke occupied Guayama on August 5, after a slight skirmish with the Spanish forces. On August 12, when he was about to launch an offensive on the slopes of Guamaní, word arrived of the armistice arranged between Spain and the United States.[35]

On August 1, Clotilde Santiago, a Coamo merchant and owner of vast tracts of land—whose son Florencio Santiago had become mayor of Coamo under the banner of the Unconditionally Spanish Party—met in Ponce with General Stone, who was in command of the city. Santiago proposed to sell the Army 500 head of cattle in Santa Isabel, and suggested that the troops detour through Salinas to take the old town of Coamo without having to test the Spanish defenses on the Central Highway. He reported that there were 1,000 Spanish troops in Coamo and 4,000 in Aibonito. While the father was conducting business with the Americans, the son was playing host in Coamo to the commander of the Spanish troops. Later *La Correspondencia* would report, with its characteristic unctiousness, that "The only municipal employees who remained firmly at their posts when the Americans marched into Coamo were the Mayor, don Florencio Santiago, and the Secretary, don Manuel Márquez, who are still discharging their duties."[37]

On the Central Highway, the Spaniards put up a brief but vigorous resistance to the enemy forces advancing from Juana Díaz. Once Coamo was secured, Wilson gathered troops and matériel, and pretended to proceed towards Aibonito, while in reality giving Brooke time to advance from Guayama to Cayey. The plan called for Brooke to occupy Cayey, forcing the Spanish to relinquish Aibonito, and once this was accomplished, Wilson's and Brooke's columns were to move forward together toward Caguas and San Juan.[38]

At the same time, Miles was planning to dislodge the scant Spanish forces that were left in the central and western parts of the island. General Roy Stone, together with some 30 soldiers, mostly from the signal corps, and several dozen *criollos* who were anxious to put an end to Spanish domination, took possession of Adjuntas on August 2. The following morning they descended to take Utuado. Stone had orders to open up the road between Adjuntas and Utuado. A brigade commanded by General Henry was to march down that road on its way to Arecibo.[39]

The most violent encounters between American and Spanish forces took place in western Puerto Rico. The three regular regiments that participated in the invasion saw action under General Schwan. The town of San Germán had lived through days of anxiety as it experienced succesive occupations by bands of civilians and Spanish troops which had returned. The mayor contacted the Americans at Yauco and urged them to seize San Germán forthwith, to free the city from the anarchy it seemed destined to suffer. Troops from General Schwan's brigade occupied the town on August 10. From there they continued on to Mayagüez in pursuit of the Spanish troops.[40]

The latter had few alternatives. If they remained in Mayagüez, they ran the risk of being trapped between the vessels of the United States fleet and the American troops. On the other hand, bands of *criollos* were beginning to spring up in the western area, with the purpose of harassing the Spanish soldiers. The option they did have was to regroup in Lares all the manpower available in the west and to delay General Schwan's combat operation, for they expected that Schwan, after ridding the west of Spanish troops, would march towards Arecibo to join with General Henry's forces. The Spanish engaged the Americans in battle near Hormigueros, and after sustaining the loss of one man and nine wounded, they retreated toward Las Marías. Schwan then occupied Mayagüez without opposition.

The Spanish were forced to fight under disadvantageous conditions on August 13, after the armistice had been decreed, because the Guasio river was swollen. The combatants did not receive the news on time. This battle turned out to be the most important one of the whole campaign. Spanish casualties amounted to five dead and 14 wounded. Fifty-six men either were taken prisoner or surrendered. When word of the armistice reached him, Schwan was planning to eliminate the rest of the Spanish forces in the area and extend his sphere of action toward Lares and Aguadilla. His casualties in the campaign were one dead and 16 wounded.[41]

Between July 25 and August 12, the military operations of the troops under Wilson, Brooke and Henry had aimed at the flank of the scant regular Spanish forces on the south side of the island. The support that the Puerto Rican population gave the invaders was crucial. Auxiliary forces made up of men on horseback, volunteers on foot, mule drivers, suppliers, guides, interpreters, harbor pilots and stevedores carried out vital functions that resulted in a smooth military operation. Puerto Rican youths, such as Carlos Patterne and Rafael Larroca, carried out dangerous missions behind Spanish lines in order to obtain military intelligence for the Americans; but, above all, it was the enthusiasm of the throngs in town after town that gave a feeling of confidence and security to the invading troops, and convinced the Spaniards they could not retain the island.[42]

How the Invasion Was Interpreted at the Time

The resounding success of the American invasion required explaining, since it stood in such stark contrast to the bitterness and anguish of the expedition to Santiago de Cuba. Ever since, the events of 1898 in Puerto Rico have seen no shortage of interpreters. What had happened and why were twin questions whose answers were soon to be framed in such a way that the one depended upon the other.

It is interesting to note the substantial shift that occurred in the American interpretation of the events of 1898 in Puerto Rico. The newspaper account that prevailed at first, as disseminated by the Associated Press, was that the invasion had been a "picnic" because Puerto Ricans had enthusiastically welcomed the troops that came to release them from the yoke of Spanish bondage. The towns asked to be occupied quickly. The Spanish, realizing they lacked support, retreated to entrenched positions in the mountains of Aibonito and Guayama. Even though the American military forces time and again gave proof of the inexperience of its volunteers, they managed to advance easily, with the cooperation of the Puerto Rican people who showed them the way, provided them with supplies, and made suitable places for setting up camp available to them. The success of the invasion was due to the cooperation of the *criollos* and the vulnerability of the Spanish forces, rather than the thrust of the Federal Army.[43]

This interpretation, of course, did not satisfy the generals. For them the success of the invasion was due to the painstaking care that Miles and his officers had taken to plan all the important aspects of the expedition to "Number Two." If the invasion had been a "picnic," it was due to the military genius of its organizers.[44]

Richard Harding Davis, the well-known novelist and war correspondent, who had been one of the two journalists present during the first wave of the invasion, and therefore, responsible for the initial interpretation, did not take long to adopt the version that favored officialdom. By Christmas, 1898, when the market for books about the recently-concluded war was at its peak, Davis had a book about his war experiences ready.

In it, Miles and the other officers received all the credit for the success of the invasion of Puerto Rico:

> In comparison to the Santiago nightmare, the Porto Rican campaign was a *fete de fleurs*. . . Porto Rico was a picnic because the commanding generals would not permit the enemy to make it otherwise. The Spaniards were willing to make it another nightmare—they were just as ready to kill in Porto Rico as in Cuba—but our commanding general in Porto Rico was able to prevent their doing so. . . The reason the Spanish bull gored our men in Cuba and failed to touch them in Porto Rico was entirely due to the fact that Miles is an expert matador. . . This is not saying that it was not a picnic, but explaining why it was so. . . An eyewitness of both campaigns must feel convinced that the great success of the one in Porto Rico was not due to climatic advantages and the cooperation of the natives, but to good management and good generalship.[45]

Some of the soldiers that took part in the marches and countermarches of the campaign had a different story to tell. For them, military organization had been criminally deficient. The lack of adequate supplies, the time it took to debark in Arroyo, negligence in the health services, the insistence that heavy uniforms be worn in the tropical summer, slow communications, the lack of experience of volunteer officers and pointless marches had been the hallmarks of the military campaign in Puerto Rico. In September, soldiers from the 3rd Illinois Volunteer Regiment, quartered in Guayama and eager to return to the States, declared to *The Chicago Daily News* correspondent that the hardships of the campaign had been the harsh camp life and the myriad diseases for which the Army had hardly prepared. One of the regiment's doctors was court-martialed for hospitalizing what was deemed to be an excessive number of soldiers. He was acquitted, which apparently angered General Grant, who was in command of that brigade. Soldiers of the 3rd Illinois also revealed to the press the arbitrariness of the higher officers, as well as the incredible shortage of rations, which impelled *The Chicago Daily News* to proclaim on its front page: "Starvation prevails in 3d Illinois at Guayama, Porto Rico."[46]

Illinois troops encamped near Ponce

Of course, the soldiers tended to exaggerate their capacity to endure hardship. Corporal Charles B. Wagner, of the 3rd Illinois "D" Company, in a letter written to his mother August 10, spun a mythical tale that was not backed by the official documentation of his brigade:

> We were under fire all day and all night and all we had to eat in the twenty-four hours was two oranges apiece. . . Our regiment's loss is twenty-nine killed and fourteen wounded. In one of the towns we captured I spotted a Spaniard on top of a three-story house aiming at one of our officers. I "nailed" him in the head and he fell down into the street.[47]

In fact, the 3rd Illinois did not lose a single man in action in Puerto Rico, although it did suffer many casualties due to typhoid fever. When Carl Sandburg wrote his reminiscences of the efforts of "C" Company of the 6th Illinois Regiment, he preferred to cast them in an ironic tone. Refuting Richard Harding Davis' "fete de fleurs" opinion, he wrote about the Puerto Rico campaign:

Mud and mosquitoes are not roses and poinsettias. Nor is sleeping in
the rain and marching in a baking sun carrying fifty pounds a feast.
Few are the picnics where they eat from baskets holding canned
beans, hardtack, and "Red Horse" and then they take off their shirts
and pluck out "seam squirrels." Dicky Davis lived with the high commanding officers. . .[48]

Five graduates of Princeton's Class of '98 enlisted in the 1st Volunteer
Engineers Regiment and went to Puerto Rico in August 1898. Shortly
after returning to the United States, two died from diseases contracted
during the campaign. The other three recounted their war experiences to
their classmates when they were getting ready to celebrate their fifth
graduation anniversary in 1903. For them, the memorable thing about the
campaign was the disorganization of the health, food and transportation
services.[49]

Similar testimony was offered by Anthony Fiala, a member of
Troop "C" of the New York Volunteer Cavalry. Conditions aboard the
"Massachusetts"—the vessel that transported the troop to Guánica—were
unbearable. The soldiers were crowded together, drinking hot, dirty water,
without hot meals, and sleeping in cramped spaces:

> The accomodations were bad and sanitary arrangements vile; the
> expedition was dispatched with such haste and so many troops were
> on board that comfort was out of the question. A place had been
> planned where the soldiers could wash, but there was no time for its
> completion, and in the early mornings when the sailors would wash
> down the quarter deck, the only luxury on board was to strip and
> jump into the stream of salt water.[50]

These and other accounts from individual participants had little impact
upon the versions of the war that were soon to predominate. One reason
why the story took another tack was the direction followed by public
debate between imperialists and anti-imperialists in 1898–99 in the
United States. Imperialists were in favor of annexing Hawaii, the
Philippines, Puerto Rico and, if possible, Cuba. Anti-imperialists felt that

the institutions of the republic would be in danger if the United States became a colonial empire, in the manner of France and Great Britain. Neither side contemplated the possibility that the annexed territories become part of the federal union.

Among the anti-imperialists, the tendency was to believe that the triumph in Puerto Rico was achieved easily because Spain had put up little resistance:

> From the debarkation at Ponce, to the occupation of the insular capital, there was nothing that could be called a war. The islanders submitted with equanimity to the invasion—to the substitution of the control of the United States over the incapable government of Spain. The majority of the people, perfectly indifferent to the ownership of the island, simply desired to be left alone. The conquest was complete with the mere appearance of the United States forces. We wanted the island; Spain was powerless to hold it, and it was ours.[51]

Such an interpretation annulled the efforts made by Miles and the other officers to underscore their organizational talents, and was in agreement with the version already suggested by war correspondent Stephen Crane in his narrative on the taking of the town of Juana Díaz.[52] The natives' indifference toward their eventual fate was easier to fit into an anti-imperialist interpretation of the war, whereas their enthusiastic participation was not. The latter could present the problem of what exactly the Puerto Ricans were trying to achieve when they helped to defeat and expel the Spaniards.

For the imperialists, however, as long as the peace treaty between Spain and the United States was under consideration in the Senate, it seemed important to underscore the willingness of Puerto Ricans to aid the Americans. Once over this hurdle, the tendency—which would become the received tradition—was to minimize the importance of Puerto Rican collaboration in the war, just as was done with that of the Cubans. Thus, there was no proof that political debts had been contracted with the people of Puerto Rico.[53]

The Invaded

On June 8, 1898, at 8 in the evening, in a warehouse belonging to the Sureda family of Utuado, "great throngs of people" responding to the summons of the mayor, the district court judge, the parish priest, the municipal judge, the district attorney, the lieutenant of the *Guardia Civil* and the Utuado municipal attorney, assembled to create and install a Local Defense Committee. "Of all the great and important meetings held in this town to deal with the present circumstances and take whatever steps are necessary to keep this territory and this district intact," this one, according to a correspondent, "turned out to be the greatest and most important." Mayor José Lorenzo Casalduc, Father Francisco García, Attorney Felipe Casalduc-Goicoechea, Doctor Manuel Quevedo-Baéz— a physician and "pure" autonomist leader—all addressed the crowd. "The people responded with joy and enthusiasm to the patriotic exhortations of the speakers." The committee was established, and all the town's citizens became members "to defend the interests of the upstanding Spaniards of Utuado in general."[54]

This marvelous concord of all the leading members of Utuado's economic and political sectors was put to the test on August 3, when the invaders—against whom the Defense Committee had been constituted in June—marched into Utuado. These amounted to some 30 soldiers under General Roy Stone, escorted into town by several dozen riders who were members of the most prominent local families. All along Comercio Street (soon renamed General Stone Street, now Dr. Cueto Street) about 5,000 persons, according to Stone's probably self-serving calculations, cheered the arrival of the invaders. The most prominent *criollo* families hung garlands across the street. The officers were invited to dances in the homes of the well-to-do. And José Lorenzo Casalduc, the same mayor who had presided over the creation of the Local Defense Committee, sent a warm message to General Miles in August:

> . . . this district shall owe a debt of eternal gratitude to the Goverment
> of the American Union and to its illustrious General Stone, who was
> the first person to raise the Stars and Stripes over this town.[55]

Now then, what is the historian to make of these two testimonies? What can he surmise about Utuado's elite, which bubbles over with patriotic prose in defense of the Spanish territory in June and then, with the same fervor, proclaims in August its allegiance to the Stars and Stripes? What is one to believe about these mayors, judges and district attorneys, who, first under one, then another political system perorated and prospered?

A simple reading might give rise to the following logical options: 1) They were sincere in June and hypocritical in August. 2) They were hypocritical in June and sincere in August. 3) They were neither sincere in June nor in August. 4) They were as sincere in June as in August, and in each instance they perceived the situation in an intense and particular manner.

The historian, however, does not have many reasons to question people's motivations. In any case, the sincerity issue is not a subtle enough key to understand the rejection of Spain and the welcoming of the Americans, a drama that was being played out in Utuado as well as other municipalities throughout the invasion.

What had occurred and what interpretation of events could take shape in so short a period of time?

There is an incident, alongside the invasion, that can serve as a starting point for reflection. Early in August, 1898, before the armistice, Captain F. W. Rodgers, of the U.S.S. "Puritan," sent a handful of men ashore to reactivate the Fajardo lighthouse, which had been out of commission since the beginning of the war. Dr. Santiago Veve-Calzada—owner of one of the largest tracts of land in the district of Ceiba, which had just recently become part of Fajardo—convinced the captain to send a detachment to occupy Fajardo. Years later, Esteban López, the Fajardo physician, collected his impressions in an intimate memoir:

> . . . one afternoon at three, the town of Fajardo was invaded by 13 United States Marines in the company of Dr. Santiago Veve, who had told them to come down into town and lower the Spanish flag that flew over City Hall, and to raise the Stars and Stripes.
>
> It was said that the invited naval officer was unwilling, because those were not his orders, but that he acceded to the doctor's

repeated entreaties and to his assurances that all the residents desired it (this was not true, as not all of us were pro-Yankee) and that besides, there would be no danger, because the Spaniards had left us.

I was extremely upset because I was never a sympathizer, and I truly regretted changing nationalities; I loved Spain, was never a separatist, and even though I detested the Spanish Governments in Puerto Rico, I loved my mother country, my Hispanic-Latin heritage, my Roman Catholic religion, my language—so rich—in which I think, in which I entrust myself to God and pray for the deliverance of my soul and that of this poor land of mine.

From the balcony of my home I witnessed the arrival of the 13 . . . soldiers. . . I also witnessed the enthusiasm of some native sons of Fajardo (who would have cheered the arrival of the Zulus with the same enthusiasm) acclaiming the Yankees, the Americans from the Continent, without knowing them or whether they would treat us better or worse that those departing.

After a brief occupation, however, the Americans had to choose to abandon Fajardo, because they did not have enough men on the "Puritan" to resist the approaching Spanish troops. Desperation then spread rapidly among those who had cheered the invaders on:

> When the news of the officer's response became known, to the effect that they could not spare any troops to leave behind in Fajardo, a panic spread throughout the neighborhood that would have provoked laughter, if only the situation had allowed it. Some scenes were quite funny. Many who had boasted they would eat the Spaniards alive had to calm their nerves with potassium bromide and bismuth; others, with rum. . .
>
> The following afternoon the Spanish troops arrived, went directly to City Hall, lowered the American flag and raised the Spanish standard amidst thundering hurrahs that were repeated by the crowd, which no doubt included a few people that hours earlier had cheered the other forces. Wretched humanity!!. . .[56]

If you will, the Fajardo example is the other side of the Utuado coin. The arriving Americans are embraced enthusiastically, the panic-stricken collaborators disband when the occupation fails, and the Spanish return, with the dreaded "Patria" battalion:

> Fortunately for Fajardo, among the troops there were some officers and companies which had been quartered here before and they knew us . . . Still, some excesses were committed . . .

Both in Utuado and in Fajardo the American occupation was promoted by a group of anti-Spain youths from prominent *criollo* families. In both cases this elite mobilized the masses to acclaim the Americans and reorganized the municipal administration to set up its own political program. The American occupation of Utuado was followed by acts of retaliation against economically powerful Spaniards. When the Spaniards re-occupied Fajardo, there followed arrests, robberies and vandalism directed against the property of United States sympathizers. These personal revenges and acts of retaliation reveal pre-existing rifts within the elite and between the elite and the masses.

It would be superficial to interpret Puerto Rican allegiance to the United States and rejection of Spain in 1898 in terms of loyalties and feelings. Young professionals who had been educated in the United States and Europe, *criollos* who owned businesses or tracts of land and were most impatient with the political regime, and sectors of the working masses in social or labor conflicts with those in leadership positions had different reasons to desire a change in the political order. But the invasion was the juncture that brought them together to welcome the Americans and reject the Spaniards. Then they saw themselves as redeemers of their country. A Mayagüez newspaper expressed it in these terms in October 1898:

> The Americans came, we believe, and so believes the country, in truth the whole country, to deliver us from the yoke of a cursed and denigrating oppression, and it was our duty, bearing in mind that a labor of love should be paid back in kind, to lend them all the assistance necessary to put an end to the presumption and the grand posturing of a great many of the demoralized and ambition-ridden Spaniards residing in these latitudes.[57]

The writer and medical doctor Manuel Zeno-Gandía, who, years later, would write a novel with the ironic title *Redentores* (The Redeemers), was among those who jubilantly celebrated the end of the old order. Zeno wrote a letter to Miles dated August 13, 1898, to tell him he had been the medical director of the port of Ponce since 1882, but that in July, "due to his well-known pro-American sympathies, he had been forced to leave the island."[58] At this early date people had neither the perspective nor the desire to differentiate between the rejection of the old order and the acceptance of the newly imposed order.

On July 25, 1899, on the first anniversary of the invasion, Evaristo Izcoa-Díaz, one of the first journalists to remark upon the contradictions of American military government policy, wrote this:

> We who are admirers of the wise institutions of the American people, and who had to bear the burden of a tyrannical regime, we believed that the descendants of Jefferson had plunged into the hazards of war in the name of oppressed humanity, and that they would come to our land to broadcast the irrefutable voice of Universal Rights. We received them with enthusiasm. We opened our doors to them. We aided them in their triumphs . . . That was yesterday. Today . . . let us not dwell upon details that the people of Puerto Rico know only too well.[59]

It is in this context of rejection of the old Spanish order that the raids of seditious bands, the *tiznados*, took place in 1898–99, and that several sectors entered into conflict with the new American order.

CHAPTER THREE

Activities of the Armed Bands from July to October, 1898

According to the stipulations agreed to by the peace negotiators, Spain was to leave Puerto Rico before signing the peace treaty with the United States. A joint committee of Spanish and American officers designed a schedule for the surrender of the municipalities, which would culminate on October 18 with the transfer of San Juan. Even though that part of the agreement was adhered to without serious problems, the transition period between the armistice on August 12 and the final departure of the Spanish authorities was beset with trouble.

During that period, different regions of the island experienced a political vacuum. The Spanish State, which had, with much difficulty, managed to rule in the farthest and most troublesome areas of the country, was dismantled. The new American political and military apparatus replacing it, however, started off by wielding its power in a hesitant, uneven manner.

Both the Spanish and the Americans confronted countless difficulties in trying to govern the Puerto Ricans during those months, particularly after the armistice of August 12. In the zone that was in Spanish hands at the time of the armistice, there were many armed bands operating in open rebellion against the government in San Juan. Many soldiers and volunteers deserted their garrisons and joined the multitude of fugitives, vagabonds and wanderers who roved the country's highways and roads. Since Admiral Sampson's bombardment in May, a large number of public officials had deserted the capital, and, having sought safety in Guaynabo,

Río Piedras or Bayamón, hesitated to return to their posts.[1] Others hastened to resign and return to Spain, hoping that by arriving home before their peers it would be easier to find a new job.

The town councils barely hid their disloyalty to the Spanish government. On August 18, Captain DeFuniak and a few soldiers of the 1st Kentucky Cavalry Regiment announced that they had occupied Aguada, and with the consent of the mayor raised the flag of the United States. That night, some 30 *Guardias Civiles* sent by the Spanish authorities in Aguadilla occupied Aguada and took Mayor Antonio Sánchez into custody. In the melee that ensued, the guards fired into the crowd, killing two civilians. The mayor was arrested and sent to San Juan, but before reaching Bayamón he escaped. The incident caused much tension between the Americans and the Spaniards.[2]

In the southern zone, occupied by the United States, the difficulties were of another sort, but they also made the functioning of the basic institutions of government quite slow. The invading forces had installed provisional mayors in a few municipalities, but these did not know the conventional way of conducting business. Most of the pre-invasion mayors were still in office, but not all were able to count on the loyalty of their employees or the cooperation of the public. Many people stopped paying taxes, with the result that it became hard to meet payrolls. Municipal and civil guards, fearful of retaliation and reprisals, abandoned their posts. Conflicts between mayors and American officers in charge of local detachments became more and more frequent because their respective functions under the military government were not clearly spelled out. The municipal assembly in Ponce in particular, which thought that it had achieved more autonomy under General Henry, governor of the military district, than it had under Spanish domination, was soon frustrated in its plans to implement its fiscal and administrative policies.[3]

General Miles had decreed that the country should go on being governed under the same laws and institutions as before unless they were in open contradiction with the Constitution of the United States. In criminal cases, however, the courts followed traditional procedure, which clashed with American sensibilities. This sometimes gave rise to conflicts between the judges and military authorities. The sudden separation of church and state also led to conflicts in the operation of social agencies which had up to that time been run by priests and nuns.[4] On the other hand, discipline was beginning to break down among American volunteer troops, who were eager to return home and resume civilian life. In the streets and plazas, incidents between civilians and drunken soldiers became more frequent. The problem of exchanging the local currency for dollars was becoming acute. Coffee wholesalers refused to extend credit so that the coffee growers could pay the harvesters unless they were guaranteed what was considered to be excessive interest.[5] There were delays in the organization of a new school year.

A swarm of adventurers, publicists and hustlers from the United States was descending on Ponce and Mayagüez.[6] The tone of relations between military officers and both local and stateside journalists was increasingly sharp. For its part, Washington made recommendations and suggestions to its military officers, which they, faced with what they perceived to be the real circumstances of Puerto Rico, found inapplicable. The schedule by which the Spanish transferred municipal power forced the American army to disperse its most capable officers throughout the territory. Competent and honest interpreters were needed because those available translated badly and were occasionally accused of acting in a biased manner.[7]

It was in these circumstances, both in Spanish-administered territory and American-occupied zones, in which the phenomenon known as seditious bands or *tiznados* occurred.

Prior History of Armed-Band Activity

Before the Spanish-American War broke out, the newspapers would occasionally mention bands of armed men who held up farms and isolated country stores.[8] Once the war began and rural policemen had to be concentrated in the district capitals, the problem of maintaining law and order in the countryside worsened. On May 30, *El País* reported a gang robbery in Barrio del Real near Ponce. On July 9, *La Unión* carried a brief description of the arrest of eight individuals in Barrio Hatillo, Añasco, for gang robbery.[9]

Public opinion attributed such incidents to the serious economic crisis that Puerto Rico was undergoing since the American blockade had paralyzed commerce, and to the prevailing uncertainty. This discouraged investment in agriculture, and as a result employment of day laborers decreased. Municipal governments tried to counteract these effects by generating activities in the areas of public works and private construction. In Ponce, for example, Mayor Ulpiano Colón suggested to the town council on July 4, 1898, that "in order to provide employment for the members of the working class, so that they may earn a living under the present circumstances . . . that the citizenry be granted permits free of charge to carry out all kinds of home improvement work during a period of six months." The council sent the proposal to a committee, where it died.[10]

A group of residents of Adjuntas petitioned Secretary of the Interior Luis Muñoz Rivera asking that the road construction project in Adjuntas be reactivated, in order to provide employment for many wage earners who would otherwise be without an income.[11] But the very crisis that the country was undergoing affected its revenues, forcing the government to reduce its expenditures.

Armed Groups That Aided the Invaders

One of Miles' justifications for invading through Guánica rather than Fajardo had been that its proximity to Yauco would favor the recruitment of bands of Puerto Rican auxiliaries. To coordinate these he was counting on the assistance of Antonio Mattei-Lluveras and Mateo Fajardo.[12]

From Guánica, General Guy V. Henry sent a memo on this subject to Adjutant General Gilmore on July 28, 1898. Gilmore was in charge of communications for Miles' high command. Henry pointed out that several residents of mountain communities had come down to Yauco that day to offer their services as soldiers and guides to the United States Army. In exchange, the Army would provide them with rations. Henry accepted the offer to send a group of these mounted volunteers, together with a few soldiers, to bring some Mauser rifles that were stored 16 miles from

Yauco.[13] Some argue that one of these "volunteers" was José Maldonado, the famous "Aguila Blanca," who, the following summer, would display a license to carry firearms signed at the time by Henry.[14]

Whether authorized by the Americans or not, bands of armed men on horseback harassed the Spanish forces and aided General Miles' troops until the day of the armistice. The commander of one of the bands had this to report to General Henry on August 1:

> Sir: In the night of yesterday, July 31, I took possession of the City of San Germán in the name of the glorious American Army. The mayor received me courteously and we went to the City Hall as they had not any police to keep the order in case it would be necessary. I immediately ordered six of my men for that purpose. I do not need to say that although it was past 10 o'clock the people all the families received me with the same content at Guanica, Yauco and Sabana Grande [*sic*]. I returned last night and now, eight o'clock a.m. I leave again for that place with all my men which number fifty. I will collect some more over there to the number of (100) one hundred. I have put some men to fix up the telegraph wire to able the communication to be reestablished. I will reestablish the mail service.[15]

Julio Tomás Martínez Mirabal wrote in his memoirs about his participation in the auxiliary party that went from Ponce with General Roy Stone to take Adjuntas and Utuado. Correspondence between Stone and Miles' headquarters shows what an important part this auxiliary troop played in the occupation of Jayuya, in patrolling the area's roads, and in obtaining supplies.[16]

On August 6, a large party of mounted men—mostly from Utuado—charged with aiding the American military forces in the district of Lares left unpaid a bill totaling 51 pesos at the home of Andrés Delgado, in Barrio Angeles, for the following items: a 375 lb. steer, priced at 45 pesos, 25 lbs. of raw sugar, 12 lbs. of inferior-grade coffee, and one peso's worth of garlic, peppers and cumin seed. Days later Delgado also made available to the band two horses and a mule, with saddles, and some cane sugar syrup "to attend the needs of these American forces that are concentrated in this area."[17] Unable to obtain payment from the Americans for the provisions or the unreturned animals, Delgado sued his customers for swindling.

On August 7, thwarted in their purpose to proceed towards Lares, the same band took part in a notorious ride that stopped two blocks short of the main plaza in Arecibo.[18] According to Dr. Pedro Hernández Paralitici, the group has gone down in Utuado's oral history as the "turkey band" for that was the trophy that they brought back to Utuado.

The Ciales Case

One of these operations came to a tragic end. The Spanish military forces had abandoned the town of Ciales.[19] The day after the armistice, that is, August 13, two bands of *criollos* occupied the town and raised the flag of the United States over the city hall. An auxiliary force of pro-Spanish volunteers arrived from Manatí on the afternoon of the same day in order to re-occupy Ciales. An armed confrontation ensued, with unfortunate results for the local group. The skirmish and the occupation of the town produced eight deaths.

Those deaths caused great uneasiness both in Ponce and in the capital. In San Juan, the government had printed and distributed copies of a clarification by the Ciales town council, which answered the charge that there were more than 100 dead. At the same time, responsibility for the deaths was attributed to local armed bands. A copy of the declaration was sent to American military headquarters. After Ciales was turned over to the Americans, the people who had signed the proclamation sent a letter to the newspapers declaring that they had signed under duress.[20] Miles also received a report written by Rodulfo Figueroa, a leader in the combat at Ciales:

> To General Miles:
> The undersigned wishes to apprise you of the following facts:
> Saturday, that is the day before yesterday, when the volunteer
> Spanish forces had retreated from *Ciales,* the townspeople

pronounced themselves in favor of the United States, whose flag they raised above city hall.

But the same day in the afternoon, at 3 o'clock, the aforementioned volunteer troops returned, joined by the volunteers from *Manatí*, all of whom, taking positions behind the cemetery, aimed their fire towards the town, which is said to have suffered much damage. Previously they had lowered the American flag, which they tore up and stepped on.

The same day, the undersigned was on the way to *Ciales* with fifty men, joined along the way by other men who also wanted to pursue the miscreants and fugitives who are indulging in all manner of excesses in that area, when a band of about fifty men bearing a Spanish flag was encountered on the road some two hours away from Ciales. In the exchange of gunfire, the Spanish casualties were about four dead and several wounded, and their flag was taken, after which they retreated and dispersed into the nearby hills.

When the undersigned arrived in the vicinity of Ciales, seeing that the enemy forces that had taken cover behind the cemetery were far superior in number, and that it was already 5 o'clock, he positioned his forces behind a small cart and opened fire, which was returned by the volunteers; Figueroa lost a horse, the one Pascasio Fernández was riding, which was felled by two bullets, and another horse belonging to Manuel Budet was wounded in the nose. Both men are members of the force under the command of the undersigned.

All cartridges spent, and having received word that more Spanish forces were on the way, it was necessary to retreat towards Ponce. At this time, a resident of that area came and said that the Spaniards were tying up the dead so as to be able to say that Figueroa had shot defenseless men.

There is a peninsular Spaniard running loose around the countryside together with a bunch of outlaws, who is using the name of the undersigned in his raids.

Besides the flag, I confiscated from the forces I met on the road to Ciales two Remingtons (rifles) and a short carbine, which I have stored.

The flag I have the honor of presenting with this letter.

Mr. Antonio Olivieri from Limón farm in Juana Díaz sent three *guardias civiles* with a patrol—Hilario Chicano, Antonio Priego-Navas and Carlos Rodríguez—who had come from Aibonito and turned up, without weapons, at his farm.

With this report I hand over to you the three aforementioned guards.

Ponce, August 15, 1898

[signed] Rodulfo Figueroa[21]

Pro-Spanish Bands of Auxiliaries

In the letter quoted above it becomes clear that there were armed bands that aided and abetted the Spanish forces. Elsewhere on the island, Spanish nationals and their Puerto Rican adherents took part in patrol operations, which did not cease when the armistice was proclaimed. For example, Esperanza Mayol, in her autobiography, describes how Matías Ferrer organized all the Majorcans in the town of Adjuntas to defend their common interests during this period.[22] On August 20, 1898, the mayor of Sabana Grande, Pablo Pietri, wrote General Schwan:

> Since rumors have reached this town that guerrillas and *Guardia Civil* forces are operating in its environs and may attempt to duplicate what happened in Ciales, the residents, foreseeing that such an attack could have deadly consequences, have approached me pleading that I request from you a force of 100 men, because this town is completely defenseless and at the mercy of anyone who desires to bring mourning and weeping to its streets, squares and fields.[23]

In San Sebastián, even after the armistice was signed, the volunteers continued to serve the Spanish government, since this zone, bordering the one occupied by the United States Army, was home to a large number of people of anti-Spanish sentiment. Nevertheless, when it became known that Spain would cede Puerto Rico to the United States, the armed bands that aided the Spaniards ceased operating. Still, on December 9, alarm spread in Maricao when several Spanish youths, who had partaken too freely of drink, paraded one evening to the sound of a military bugle.[24] Furthermore, on occasion during September and October the *criollos* tried to place the blame for holdups and the burning down of haciendas on armed bands of Spaniards.

Were There Pro-Independence Bands?

For the period between the invasion by the American army on July 25 and the formal installation of the military government in San Juan on October 18, 1898, none of the existing documents consulted bears witness to activities by bands whose avowed purpose was to obtain independence for Puerto Rico or to resist the installation of the American regime on the island.

The members of the Junta of Puerto Ricans in New York who traveled to Puerto Rico during that period all cooperated with the American forces. So did all the bands of anti-Spanish Puerto Ricans who have been identified so far.

In recent times there has been an attempt to cast the activities of José "Aguila Blanca" Maldonado, in pro-independence terms. In chapter 5 below there is a section on Aguila Blanca that examines his activities during 1898–99 in another light.

From Bands of Auxiliaries to "Tiznados"

During the weeks following the invasion it was quite evident that people were in a mood to settle scores with the Spaniards. In Ponce, the multitude turned against those pro-Spanish volunteers who had laid down their arms and accepted the terms of surrender. They were hauled to the public square by force:

> Bloodhounds could not have been more savage. Most of the Spaniards in hiding, upon being discovered, were hailed in triumph by hooting, jeering mobs to Gen. Wilson's headquarters or to the Provost Marshal's Office in the municipal buildings. Some of the natives even began looting the residences of the Spaniards.[25]

In the towns it was relatively easy for the Americans to contain these outbursts of violence. Partly for this reason, most of the attacks against the persons and property of the Spaniards took place in the countryside.

Already after the taking of Yauco it had been feared that the *criollos* would loot, kill, and destroy property in the rural areas, in retaliation for "the many years of bad Spanish government."[26]

This mood to settle scores, together with the need for food among the peasants and the laborers in the highlands, was responsible for the first sorties of the armed bands.

On August 8, *La Correspondencia* reported that out in the country near Ciales

> a peaceful group has been formed—since it carries no weapons— made up of some 70 men, who go to the farms of the well-to-do ask- ing for something to eat. They visited Mr. Lorenzo Joy, the wealthy owner of Cialitos, who ordered a heifer killed for them, and with 100 lbs. of rice an abundant feast was prepared, which they dispatched with vigor and determination. Afterwards they departed amidst cheers for Mr. Joy and his family.[27]

As the bands that had been forming in the highlands began to need sup- plies, they would go to the farmers and merchants in the area to request food. But the typical band in search of food did not behave in this idyllic manner. As often as not the members killed and consumed an animal in the open fields, or they took possession of the stock of rice or corn meal from the hacienda store without any formalities.[28]

Once the armistice was proclaimed, the bands that were organized for military purposes were, by and large, dissolved. In their place we see the emergence of night raids by bands whose members blacken their faces with charcoal or cover their features in order to go unrecognized. And now what seems to motivate the *tiznados* is not so much the search for supplies to feed its members as political or economic retaliation.

One of the earliest and most notorious cases took place on the night of August 18 to 19, in a barrio of Ponce called Coto del Laurel. According to the night watchman's declaration, a large group of people arrived at the store belonging to a peninsular Spaniard, Felipe Martínez, between 10 and 11 p.m. One pointed a gun at the watchman's chest while the rest opened the store, tossed the merchandise out in the street and set fire to

Martínez's buildings. The flames reached neighboring structures and 16 or 17 houses burned down. But the throng that surrounded the place, instead of helping put out the fire, proceeded to loot. When an American military detachment arrived, they found that the people, in a festive mood, were pouring buckets of water on one another.[29]

On Friday, August 19, at 9:30 p.m., a band of 30 to 40 people showed up at Hacienda Santa Cruz, belonging to the heirs of the Castañer estate, in the municipality of Yauco. They wounded the overseer, Bartolomé Oliver, with their machetes, and burned down the farmhouse in which he lived, the machinery building and the warehouse. Oliver managed to identify 13 of his assailants.[30]

On August 25, between 9 and 10 p.m., a group of unknown individuals, "calling on behalf of American Guards" appeared at the home of Higinio Gómez, in Barrio Portillo, Adjuntas. They tore the lock off the door and stole men's and women's clothing, two watches, two gold watch chains and a saddle.[31]

By September and October 1898, isolated coffee plantations in the highlands which were the property of Spaniards had become the favorite target of these bands. They would show up after dark, some on horseback, others on foot. They would steal food from the hacienda store or the warehouse, as well as liquor, clothing, saddles, and perhaps a piece of furniture from the main house. They would threaten the overseer, the administrator, or the landowner present, and sometimes they set fire to the hacienda buildings.

The number of members who reportedly made up the bands that operated between mid-August and mid-October fluctuated between eight and 200 men. It is possible that the higher figures are an exaggeration on the part of the plaintiffs, either through miscalculation or an unwillingness to give the impression that the victims had yielded to a mere handful of men.

In most of the cases reported, the plaintiff declared he was unable to recognize any of the perpetrators because their faces were coal-blackened, because they wore a mask, or because there was insufficient light to see their faces. As a rule, when the band arrived, the house was locked up and there were no lights on. The *tiznados* banged on the doors, threw

Residence of a wealthy coffee planter

rocks, and threatened to set the house on fire if they were not allowed in. Most times the man in charge opened the door and a few band members went inside, tied up or kept an eye on the older males, instructed the women to remain in their rooms, and proceeded to loot.[32]

In some cases the landowner or his administrator sustained bodily injuries. Court records seldom give information on the rape of women. It is possible that few victims of such abuse cared to testify and be subjected to questioning. Nevertheless, the oral tradition kept alive the memory of many attacks on women.[33]

If the buildings were going to be burned, the residents of the house were escorted out. The fire was ignited with a torch or a burning rag. In some cases the assailants subjected the owner or administrator to some type of humiliation and in a very few cases, they wounded or killed him. On departing, they made menacing remarks, to the effect that the Spaniard should go home to Spain, or abandon the farm.[34]

These armed bands that operated in the coffee-growing zone during September and October of 1898 were undoubtedly moved by a desire for retaliation. The Spaniards lost the war and had to pay the consequences.

Occasionally, conflicts of an economic nature are alluded to, and a few times, reference is made to the period of the *compontes* (1887).[35]

Armed Bands in the Judicial District of Utuado

Let us examine in greater detail what happened in one of the areas that was most intensely affected by the armed bands, that is, the zone under the jurisdiction of the district court of Utuado, which at the time included Adjuntas, Ciales and Lares.

According to an accusation made afterwards, on the night of August 21 a band of at least ten men from Jayuya, armed with revolvers and machetes

> stopped Mr. Eusebio Grau and his peons Pedro "Puché" Rivera, Medero Vázquez and Ysidro Andújar, on the road known as "La Pica" and threatening grievous violence took possession of a 200 lb. load of codfish, two loads of salt of 300 boxes each, one box of 400 packs of cigarettes, a suitcase containing a change of clothes, as well as 200 pesos in cash, and one mule. The stolen provisions was [*sic*] the property of Mssrs. N. Canales and Co., the cash belonged to Mr. Julio Grau and the suitcase and clothes to Mr. Eusebio Grau.[36]

Eusebio Grau was the grandson of the *criollo* Eusebio Pérez, Jayuya's conservative political boss, and the son of Julio Grau, who administered Pérez's properties and also served as petty mayor of Jayuya. To assault him on a public road was to challenge the old order openly. Of the ten assailants identified, four were members of families that owned small properties and six were day laborers from the area. It is interesting to note that even though all were residents of that municipality (Utuado, to which Jayuya belonged), the six laborers and three of the other four persons accused had been born in other towns. Despite the upheaval brought on by the invasion, it would seem that to challenge the power of an Eusebio Pérez, it was necessary to have been born in another community, a place where such a figure had not reigned over local life for more than 40 years, as had been the case in Jayuya since the 1850s.

As in other occasions, the court in Utuado refused to entertain the case because a state of war prevailed and the case fell under military jurisdiction. In November, the commander of the military district of Ponce, General Henry, ordered the Utuado district court to proceed with the prosecution of the case. On April 8, 1899, the criminal court in Mayagüez, with José de Diego among its judges, found three of the laborers and one of the small-property owners guilty. They were sentenced to eight years, 11 months and 11 days imprisonment, and to pay damages to the victims.[37]

On August 25, between 9:00 and 10:00 p.m., a band showed up at the home of Zacarías Gómez, in Barrio Portillo, Adjuntas, "claiming to be American Guards." The residents slipped away and sought refuge with José María Delgado. Upon returning the following day, "they found the house open and everything in disarray, men's and women's outer wear missing, as well as two watches, two gold chains and a saddle." The case was never resolved in the courts.[38]

The nights of September 3 and 4, unknown individuals set fire to all the buildings on a farm in Barrio Viví Arriba, in Utuado.[39] The property owner, Pedro Castro-González, declared that, ever since Utuado had been occupied "by the American forces," he and his family had gone to live in town, leaving no one to look after his property. He had been informed of the fires by the laborers. Questioned by the authorities, the laborers accused no one. Neither could Castro identify any suspects:

> the testifier supposes that the fires were intentionally set, though he has no suspects, and he bases this supposition on the fact that the area had been rife with rumors that fires were going to be set . . . and besides, since the neighborhood was left without patrols, he had recently agreed to move with his family into town, believing they would all be safer . . .[40]

In Utuado's Barrio Mameyes, the evening of September 4, between 10 p.m. and midnight, a group of ten to 12 armed men demanded that the Spaniard Joaquín Rodríguez unlock the store he had on the ground floor of his house. Born in Santa María del Páramo, León, Spain, Rodríguez had been a member of the *Guardia Civil* in 1868 and then a store clerk for three years. In 1877, he purchased with his savings three *cuerdas* [one *cuerda* = .97 acre] of land in Mameyes and set up the first store in the area. By 1885 he had founded Hacienda Vista Alegre, which in 1896 comprised 400 *cuerdas*, 150 of them planted in coffee. At that time the hacienda included a machinery building with two tanks for washing coffee berries, a building used for selecting and processing the berries for export, a house where laborers and employees slept, a two-story building with 16 movable drying trays that could be rolled out into the sunshine, a dispatcher's booth, a two-story residence, 30 houses for laborers, stables, a lumber-storage shed, a building that housed the general store, a wooden structure that housed the neighborhood school, and a station house for the Civil Guards. Two smaller farms were dependent on the hacienda: one was "Santa Barbara" and the other "Los Montes" of 85 and 120 *cuerdas* respectively. Rodríguez also owned an 86-*cuerda* farm in Barrio Frontón, Ciales. With the exception of harvest time, the plantation owner employed 116 laborers on his farms.[41]

Rodríguez let his assailants enter and they carried off between 300 and 400 pesos worth of shoes, codfish, rice, lard, sugar, china, pots, spoons, bolts of waterproof material and various other items. Later he described the members of the band as "dark men who seemed to have their skin artificially blackened." Apparently it was the same band which, that same night, robbed a nearby farm belonging to Gaspar Homar.[42] Even though the petty mayor of Jayuya, Julio Grau, went as far as mentioning the names of suspects in both cases, the district court of Utuado refused— *motu propio*—to entertain the case and continued the proceedings until November, at which time they were reopened by order of General Henry. In spite of the depositions given by the three clerks that Rodríguez employed, and that of Mayor Grau, the investigation did not produce solid clues for the prosecution and the case was dismissed in May of 1899.[43]

According to an accusation that was made much later, on September 6, 1898, "José Alcasa, his brother Francisco Alcasa, Amelio Alicea and several unknown men gained access to the home of Narciso Sierra, raped his wife, and carried off everything that was in the house." Both José and

Narciso Alcázar died while at the Arecibo Jail, before their trial could be held. Some time later, José "Sule" Monserrate Pérez, was also charged in connection with this case. In 1900, the year the charges were filed, Narciso Sierra was the owner of 73 *cuerdas* of land in Mameyes Abajo.[44]

A 404-*cuerda* farm in Utuado's Barrio Santa Isabel, which belonged to the estate of Pedro Rullán, was the object of a raid late in the evening of September 8. Acording to Bartolomé Arbona, who represented the estate, the band members took 27 pesos worth of corn and locally-grown rice. Arbona and the people who worked in the house attacked the raiders, who retreated after shouting "Don't worry, you won't get away." They left behind two horses which turned out to belong to the owner of a small property nearby, who stated that the animals had been stolen. A resident of the area, Adelo Alicea, the only suspect named in the investigation, was never prosecuted.[45]

The night of September 14, two shots were fired by members of a band into the house of Francisco Márquez, in Barrio Bartolo, Lares. According to his testimony, the assailants, under cover of darkness, identified themselves as "Americans." Márquez retorted that they were bandits. "Don Pancho," they called, using his nickname, "open the door or you will suffer the consequences." Márquez, afraid that his dehusked coffee would be stolen, as had happened to other landowners in the vicinity, refused. The band members aimed their fire towards the door. Márquez then pretended he was not alone and shot at them from different windows. When the raiders tried to force their way through the door, Márquez shot one of them. They dispersed, leaving the wounded man behind.

The latter turned out to be Manuel Arroyo, age 20, who would later declare that he had been compelled to participate by Pablo Vélez, Pablo Ferri and Marte Morales, with another 14 to 20 men. In fact, in December Vélez and Ferri were accused of belonging to a secret society that bore the anarchistic name "La Mano Negra"—the Black Hand.[46] Based on the testimony that Arroyo gave before dying of his wound on October 4, a military commission convened in Mayagüez in April 1899 sentenced Vélez to three years in prison. He was the son of a woman who owned a small estate in Lares.[47]

In Utuado's Barrio Don Alonso, also on September 14, about 10:30 p.m., a band came to the home of Rafael Herrera Varo, an Andalusian.[48] According to his testimony, there were

> about 80 or 100 men, armed with revolvers and machetes. They banged on the door, discharged their firearms several times, and after tearing off a window, they came in demanding the keys to the hacienda store and the warehouse. The keys were handed over, and they proceeded to open them.

Among the goods stolen from Herrera that night were six hundredweights of salt, 8,000 ears of corn, two hundredweights of codfish, two hundredweights of sugar, 220 empty sacks, 84 tarpaulins, 8,000 cigars, one box of Epsom salts, 12 dozen spoons, 14 or 15 baskets for collecting coffee beans, one set of funnels and measures, oil, starch, fabrics, rum and anise. The assailants "tore up all of the store's account books," but Herrera "could not recognize any of them because almost all were disguised, that is, their faces were coal-blackened."[49]

The night of September 19, in Barrio Vegas Arriba, Adjuntas, a band of men with pack animals, claiming to belong to the police force, showed up at a farm that belonged to the Majorcan Vicente Morey Castañer. The owner was away, but his brother Antonio opened the door. Four men dressed as guards entered first, followed by a group of partisans armed with guns and rifles. Both Antonio Morey and the overseer, Antonio Barceló Mestre, who was also from Majorca, were tied up. The raiders stole clothing, bed linens, shoes, a watch, a ring, four or five pesos in cash, and rice, codfish, lard, onions, soap and rum. Then they marched the two Majorcans out of the house, tied them to trees, and set fire to the house with fuel-soaked clothing. The house burned down. The identity of the attackers was not known, but Morey described one

> . . . who had blackened his features with charcoal, but with perspiration the blackening streaked and the witness was able to observe that his natural color was white, that he was young, dressed in civilian clothes, wearing shoes and a slightly soiled jacket, short of stature, and with a scant mustache.[50]

The case was not resolved judicially.

In Barrio Guayabo Dulce, Adjuntas, on September 24, about 12 individuals showed up at the home of Jaime Oliver, fired shots in the air and threatened to set the house on fire if they were not allowed in. They carried off Oliver's provisions, and three horses. The victim thought that among his assailants were four individuals who had just the previous morning inquired where a certain neighbor lived. The neighbor, however, declared that he had been ill on that day and had not received visitors. The case did not prosper in the courts.[51]

Ulpiano Rodríguez, who lived in Barrio Guilarte, Adjuntas, filed a complaint because on the night of September 27 he had been held up by ten or 12 men who had fired seven shots. Rodríguez escaped through a window; the men broke down a door and stole money, a watch, clothing, shoes, alcoholic beverages and documents. Rodríguez did not recognize any of his assailants, but thought they were from another *barrio*. The case was never resolved in the courts.[52]

American Soldiers Intervene for the First Time

On the morning of August 19, soldiers from "K" Company, 19th Infantry Regiment and cavalry from Troop "C" of the New York Volunteers went to Coto del Laurel to try to put out a fire and stop the looting of the property belonging to Francisco Martínez. In September, a military commission found probable cause against Juan Martínez, Félix Rigau and Francisco Lanzo, who were accused of participating in the events of Coto del Laurel the night of August 18.[53] This is the first known case of military intervention in the activities of the bands.

For the military authorities, such acts were the work of "bandits." Roads and highways were not safe during those months, and even travelers were held up from time to time. In August, the area of Barros (Orocovis) was already considered unsafe.[54] Towards the end of September, a band of robbers held up the mail coach that traveled from Coamo to Ponce.[55]

The *criollos* were not the only ones responsible for such misdeeds. On

August 29, General Ernst reported to General Gilmore that two soldiers, armed with revolvers and riding native horses, had participated in a hold-up on the highway between La Playa and Ponce. The assailants claimed to be messengers from headquarters.[56] In Guayama, other soldiers held up a store and confiscated cash and goods in the name of the American occupation.[57] These and other criminal acts commited by the American volunteers placed further strain on the fragile fabric of law and order.

Hacienda owners in different parts of the zone occupied by American military forces had since August been calling for the military to protect them from the raiders. In the region of Utuado, it was common during that period—at the end of August and the beginning of September, when there were still large numbers of troops concentrated in the area—to assign a pair of soldiers to watch over the hacienda of people who so requested. Chaplain Thomas Sherman, General Miles' cousin by marriage, described one of these night watches in an article that would appear in print months later in the United States. It was about Hacienda San Gabriel, the property of José Blanco in Caonillas Abajo, in the foothills of Cerro Morales:

> Three of the civil guard [sic] arrived at supper-time armed with Remington rifles and with well-filled cartridge pouches. Lights were placed commanding the approaches to the buildings in all directions, sentries set, and we retired with our revolvers loaded and at hand. I realized then that the hacienda was in a state of siege and I gathered that the owner, a lieutenant-colonel by the way in the Spanish volunteers, was especially unpopular in the district and that the "venganza" people, as I choose to call them, had vowed his utter destruction. About midnight the dogs began to bark furiously and a single pistol shot rang out on the night air. Instantly we were out peering into the dark for dusky forms approaching. None came, but somewhat later on, the sky was lurid with the flames of a neighboring hacienda . . . Later still came the rumor of a party advancing up the mountain. I hallooed to them, and was answered in a tone quite distinctly American . . . They proved to be two soldiers, friends of Señor Blanco, who had defended his property of their own accord a few nights before and had come again to continue their work. The poor colonel embraced them as his children and then went to bed and to sleep with the utmost confidence.[58]

As the volunteer regiments began to be shipped back to the United States, however, and as Spain formally handed over the municipal governments in the middle of September, it became undesirable, from a military standpoint, to spread the small number of forces throughout the network of haciendas. These were left unprotected. That is why, in the coffee-growing zone in the center of the island, starting in the middle of September, there was an increase in the number of incidents involving armed bands.

The avalanche of complaints filed in the district courts as a result of this resurgence was so overwhelming that the courts opted to declare themselves incompetent, since, technically, a state of war prevailed on the island, and referred the files of the complaints and accusations to the headquarters of the American forces in Ponce.[59] The lack of action on the part of the judiciary in turn encouraged the frequency of the raids and the audacity of the raiders.

Given the circumstances, the military detachments that had been assigned to the municipalities began to patrol the main roads. There were soon clashes between the patrols and several armed bands. Following the suggestion of hacienda owners, the patrols carried out searches in the homes of peasants and *agregados* looking for stolen goods. The troops tried to make their visible presence the main means of discouraging the raiders. Instead of disappearing, however, the bands became more cautious and took greater care in planning their operations.

CHAPTER FOUR

The Bands, from October 1898 to February 1899

According to the terms agreed upon by a joint committee representing the United States and Spain, to carry out the transfer of powers in Puerto Rico, from the middle of September the Americans began taking control of the municipalities that were in Spanish hands. They completed the process by raising the American flag in San Juan on October 18. That day, the military government was formally established on the island.[1]

In the United States, the nature of the political statute that was to rule Puerto Rico was being debated in newspapers and public forums. An anti-imperialist sentiment had been developing around distinguished figures from the old Republican Party, like Senator Hoar of Massachusetts and ex-President Benjamin Harrison. Some leaders of the Democratic Party also shared this sentiment. Those opposed to the annexation of the Philippines, Hawaii, Guam, Cuba and Puerto Rico held a huge variety of ideas and feelings. For some, annexation jeopardized American racial unity. For others, for the United States to rule the new territories in an autocratic fashion endangered republican institutions. The exuberant rhetoric of the opponents of McKinley's new imperial policy mixed together such arguments as the dangers of the tropics, the religious differences, the need for a permanent army and the defense costs, and the natural right of the inhabitants of these islands to rule themselves.[2]

However, the easy naval victories during the war and the euphoria of success had made many politicians into expansionists. The war against

Spain seemed to have closed the old wounds of the Civil War. In the North, the bravery of Southerners during the Spanish-American War, such as those of General Wheeler and Lieutenant Hobson, were being purposely displayed, perhaps in the hope that the whole nation would close ranks behind the administration. The Congressional session ended in July 1898, amidst ardent acclamations from House members for Dewey, Sampson, Schely, Wheeler and other military leaders. For the first time, the enthusiastic members of Congress even sang *Dixie* right on the floor of the House. The annexation of territories—Hawaii's had just been completed in July—seemed to consolidate a new spirit of unity and a sense of national mission.[3]

While the pressing debate between expansionists and anti-expansionists was taking place, President McKinley exercised his faculties as Commander in Chief of the Army in the occupied territories. With these powers he appointed first John R. Brooke, and then Guy V. Henry, as military governors of Puerto Rico. However, the military government had a provisional status. As such, it postponed the solution to the already agitated problem of whether the United States would impose not only its flag but its constitution upon the islands.

In Puerto Rico, the transitory status of the military regime diminished its credibility.[4] Generals Brooke and Henry, called to confront the problem of the bands, lacked sufficient political authority to win over the Puerto Rican professional and financial sectors, whose support was essential for establishing the new order. Because of this, the bands were able to take advantage of the precarious solidarity between the military government and the influential political and financial sectors of the country.

The Bands Related to the Coffee Harvest

In the lowest regions of the coffee-growing municipalities, the coffee harvest began as early as the middle of August. In those areas, the bands coincided with the pre-harvest weeding and with the harvest itself. The hacienda owners' anxiety about the fate of the new harvest grew as October—the month in which most coffee growers began their picking—advanced.

Coffee prices had gone down in 1897. The drought during May and the excessive rains from then on had produced a mediocre harvest. It had become difficult to get credit since the beginning of the war.[5] Also, after the armistice, uncertainty about future access to the European and Cuban markets discouraged lending. Doubt about the political future of the island had slowed down the extraordinary expansion enjoyed until then by the vigorous and even exuberant economy of Puerto Rican coffee.

However, it was the 1898–99 bands which dealt the hardest blow to hacienda owners who produced, processed and consigned the coffee to be exported. The sequence was the following: reduction in prices, shrinking of credit, political uncertainty, bands, Hurricane San Ciriaco. This sequence proved devastating for the hegemony of coffee in Puerto Rico. Most of all, the bands demonstrated the precariousness of coffee haciendas.

In the first place, the bands damaged the harvest. For example, at midnight on October 23–24, 1898, a band of one hundred people raided the farm of Ledesma, Artau & Compañía, in Barrio Viví Arriba in Utuado. After taking around 30 fanegas of white-hulled coffee from the storeroom and various amounts of provisions from the store, they told overseer Ceferino Henríquez, "not to fear for the family, but he was warned that nobody should pick coffee on the farms for less than four pesos a fanega, that whoever did so would be punished, and that he should be careful to sell as his own half of what little coffee he picked."[6]

According to the charge filed later, Manuel Ríos Hernández on October 31, armed with a machete, said to the men working a coffee field belonging to Jorge Oliver in Barrio Guayabo Dulce in Adjuntas, that "if they continued picking coffee for less than five pesos a fanega, he would come back with eight or ten more men to cut them up with their machetes."[7]

On November 18, a band of 12 armed men raided the farm of Francisco Giraldez at Barrio Pellejas in Adjuntas and took the coffee that was in the washing tank. The assailants warned the overseers ". . . to stop looking after the haciendas owned by Spaniards, and that the only thing they should agree to do was to rent or go halves with the Spaniards."[8]

Another problem the hacienda owners encountered was clandestine coffee crops on their own farms. Some were brave enough to report the fact to the authorities. For example, Spaniard Tomás Pérez, the administrator of the farm belonging to Dr. Celso Caballero (from Palencia, Spain) near the town of Adjuntas, filed a report with the town's chief of police on September 23. The complaint said that María and Elena Feliciano were picking coffee on Caballero's property and that they had broken the coffee trees after picking the berries. When questioned, both women stated they were picking coffee on Lito Cardona's farm, whose overseer had given them permission to pick what they needed for that day's use. They added that the coffee trees had been broken by the heavy rains and they had not gone over to Caballero's farm. Cardona's Criollo overseer, José Palmieri, corroborated the two women's statements, and so the case was eventually dismissed.[9]

On November 8, owner Vicente Bernacet[10] from Barrio Caonillas Abajo complained to the Utuado mayor:

> because in my coffee fields . . . they have taken around two *cuerdas* [.97 acres] of ripe coffee, and as this is stealing and a crime, since I am working to fulfill my tax commitments and respond to my obligations, I request the authorities to please catch the wrong-doers and punish them as the law requires. I earnestly plead that the Authorities do not ignore my complaint; this will prevent greater abuses . . .

Bernacet calculated the stolen coffee at 5 fanegas that he estimated were worth 55 pesos. However, the adjacent neighbors said they had not heard anything about the matter. Two neighbors, called in to assess the loss, said Bernacet had only lost 3 *almudes*, or 3 half fanegas, with an estimated value of 1 peso, 50 cents. The case was not settled in court.[11]

Immediately after a band attacked Lino Vivó's property, in Barrio Don Alonso in Utuado on the night of November 15, overseer Adolfo Barbosa stated that an *agregado*, or service tenant of the property, named Cecilio Torres had been picking coffee "because he says he has the right to do so." The owner, who lived in Utuado, declared in turn that Barbosa "on dif-

A coffee-drying yard on a plantation in Puerto Rico

ferent occasions has given me notice that a man named Cecilio and other farm workers were picking coffee from the trees, and that he was constantly being harassed in his home because they threw stones at it and hit the walls with their machetes." Although some months later the authorities questioned Cecilio Torres, he was not called to a preliminary hearing and the case was dismissed.[12]

On November 27, the Criollo Santos Palmieri reported to the Municipal Judge in Adjuntas that María Eustaquia Negrón Yambó, wife of Alejandro Hernández, was picking coffee without permission at Palmieri's farm, accompanied by a boy. According to the statement of the overseer Eugenio Rodríguez Natal, the woman tried to run away when caught, but Rodríguez took her basket full of coffee. She refused to go with him to the hacienda house. When questioned, she denied that it was true and said that day she was too ill even to leave her home. Her 12-year-old son said the same thing. Summoned to appear in Mayagüez in April, María Eustaquia Negrón seems to have been found guilty, as she was

included in the pardon and amnesty for minor offenders, decreed by
Henry before he left office in May 1899.[13]

While some workers did things to claim their rights to a larger share of
profit from the crops, the small coffee growers, for their part, sought to
appropriate the coffee stored on the haciendas. There are numerous band
incidents where they took the hulled coffee from machinery houses and
storehouses. Once, they even took hulled coffee from a washing tank.
Following are the cases registered in the court files of the Utuado municipality during that period:

7 October (entry date)
Barrio Angeles. 7 *almudes* of white-husk coffee. Owners: Anastasio
and Vicente Agosto.

23 October
Barrio Viví Arriba. 30 fanegas of unhulled coffee. Owner: Ledesma,
Artau & Cía.

15 November
Barrio D. Alonso. 14 bags of white-husk coffee of 5 *almudes* ea.;
2 bags of dry-husk coffee of 5 *almudes* each. Owner: Lino Vivó.

26 November
Barrio Viví Arriba. 7 fanegas of hulled coffee. Owner: Benito Ruiz.

10 December
Barrio Viví Arriba. 2 and a half fanegas of unwashed coffee. Owner:
Benito Ruiz.

16 December
Barrio Viví Arriba. 10 fanegas of green-husk coffee. Owner: Casellas
& Ginard.

20 December

Barrio Viví Arriba. 56 *almudes* of hulled coffee, 24 *almudes* of white-husk coffee. Owner: Benito Ruiz.

23 January

Barrio D. Alonso. 13 fanegas of coffee valued at 208 pesos. Owner: Manuel Avilés.

26 January

Barrio Caonillas Abajo. 8 fanegas of dry coffee beans. Owner: Heirs of Félix Corraliza.

We must assume that the stolen coffee was sold to middlemen from Criollo business firms. Obviously, no evidence remained from these cases. Nevertheless, suspicions existed and contributed to complicating the relationship between Spaniards and Criollos of the ruling class.[14]

Some bands also robbed mule trains carrying husked coffee from the interior of the island to the coast. For example, a band seized 10 quintals of coffee from Casellas & Company that belonged to Juan Ginard. The coffee was being taken to Ponce by mule. Following is the summary of the statement of mule driver Bautista Cordero Colón, from Barrio Tibes in Ponce:

> . . . on the day mentioned the declarant was in this city [Utuado] bringing some loads to don Jesús Ramírez; and after he had unloaded, don Juan Casellas came up to him offering the declarant ten quintals of coffee to take to Ponce; which, having agreed on the cost of the trip, he loaded up and left rather late; and on arriving at the house of don Francisco Vázquez, it already being dark and the animals tired, he asked don Francisco to allow him to spend the night there and don Francisco agreed; he set the animals loose in an enclosure and . . . unloaded the ten coffee bags in a small machinery house; and told Justo Sala, a farm worker who was accompanying him, to lie down. . . . About an hour later he heard . . . someone call Vázquez and told him to bring out the load that belonged to the

Majorcans or else they would set fire to the house; Vázquez then called him and said he could not stay there any longer as he feared they would burn down the house; he understood, and again loaded up and continued his trip; but, around half an hour later a band of men armed with machetes and revolvers came toward him, and threatening him seized the packs and left, leaving only the animals. . . . The men were all blackened with charcoal and disguised, so he did not recognize them; and when he arrived at the house of don Francisco Vázquez he did not say the packs belonged to Casellas.[15]

The Bands and the Rural Trade

The bands had a particular effect on rural trade. For them, the hacienda stores were a natural target. First of all, these were stocked with food and other essential articles which were tempting to the assailants. Then, there were the store's account books in which were recorded the neighbors' debts, payable in work or crops. Finally, more than any other rural building, the stores represented the financial domination of large farmers and towns over small growers and rural workers.

Court files about the raiding and burning of stores describe in detail the losses merchants attributed to the looting of the bands. For example, Ledesma Artau & Co. declared that on October 23 a band had stolen from them 513 pesos and 95 cents, of which 450 pesos (87.6 percent) was in coffee, 41.75 (8.1 percent) in food, 9.20 in cash, and 13 pesos in store furnishings.[16]

The bands took an interest in destroying the stores' account books. A band from Barrio Guaraguao in Ponce, for example, allowed the clerk in an hacienda store belonging to Guillermo Arbona to bring out a trunk with his personal belongings before they set fire to the building. However, when they could not find the store's account books, they searched the trunk and took out the books and burned them.[17] In Cidra, a band burned the books of the House of Sariego. In this case, suspicions fell on some people from the town. As mentioned in the previous chapter, the band which stole from Rafael Herrera in Barrio Don Alonso, in September, tore up the store account books. The gang that on November 26 looted Benito

Ruiz's farm, at Viví Arriba, burned and scattered the papers found on the desk in the machinery house. These "papers were lists of farm workers and coffee accounts. No signs were found on the desk or on the floor of the entire building. There was not the least sign that a fire had occurred or that the least attempt had been made to cause one."[18]

The burning of hacienda stores was not only an act of revenge. Sometimes, better than any other symbol, it represented the long-awaited liberation from the previous socioeconomic regime. Arbona's store, mentioned above, had already been burned in August, and Arbona had set it up in another building. When the band came to loot it in October, they told the clerk and a neighbor that it was unacceptable for Arbona to set up his store again in the neighborhood.[19]

Cattle and the Bands

Although the bands' main activity zone was the coffee-growing mountain range, the *tiznados*, as band members were called because they blackened themselves with charcoal, did not stop at looting haciendas and hacienda stores, nor did they limit their activities to the mountains. Cattle, abundant in the coastal plains were an easy target for their attacks, and these were more difficult to prevent than those on the haciendas. On January 23, 1899, the northern military district commander admitted that cattle stealing continued in the western part of the Bayamón judicial district, but that it was beginning to decrease in other areas under his command.[20] However, numerous reports on the stealing, mutilation or killing of cattle show how illusory it was to say that the situation was under control.

Among the municipalities most affected were Aguadilla, Bayamón, Ciales, Dorado, Guánica, Isabela, Manatí, Mayagüez, Moca, San Sebastián, and Toa Alta. Stealing and killing cattle was considered an indication of just how poor the masses were.[21]

The Bands in the Sugar Cane Area

The activities of the "seditious" bands on sugar cane haciendas are more difficult to verify. The first sugar cane harvest after the invasion did not begin until the end of the band's most intense period of activity. Perhaps, this is why there was less opportunity for "reprisals" motivated by the invasion to coincide with the harvest's labor conflicts. Most hacienda owners during this period were Criollos and non-Spanish Europeans, so there was less justification for the attacks. In any case, it is probable that the economic and social changes in the sugar cane zone were not so recent and the experience of dispossession had been integrated into the mental perspective of the communities.

By November 1898, there were reports of problems on the sugar cane plantation of someone called Mercado, in Guayanilla. At the beginning of December, day laborers from Barrio Capitanejo in Ponce went on strike, and "fires burned in the sugar cane fields at Haciendas Fortuna, Unión, and Cristina, the latter located near Juana Díaz. There are people who, although groundlessly, attribute these acts to the strikers."[22] During January 1899, there were strikes at several sugar cane haciendas in Guayama. Troops guarded the haciendas "because fires are frequent in that jurisdiction."[23] The authorities arrested two boys and accused them of starting two fires in sugar cane fields in Guayama. The civil judge let them go, in spite of instructions sent by Henry "that the boys should be kept until frightened into telling who had incited them to start the fires in the sugar cane fields."[24] Around that time there were four attempts to start fires on Hacienda Florida, in Barrio Felicia in Santa Isabel. The hacienda was the property of Carlos Cabrera, from Ponce.[25]

The expectation of the military authorities that more fires would spring up in sugar cane fields did not materialize. At the beginning of February 1899, a sugar cane field was partially burned in Rincón, but it was not clear if the fire had been set intentionally or accidentally. There were also "some attempts to start fires on Hacienda Ana María," in Coto Laurel in Ponce. On March 15, six *cuerdas* of the Hacienda Verdegues in Guayama were burned. It is possible that fires such as the one on Jerónimo

Landrau's property in Río Piedras may have been intentional.[26] In any case, the 1899 sugar cane harvest was poor because of the uncertainty during 1898 which had discouraged investment by landowners in increasing of the amount of land cultivated and the replanting of crops.

Extortion

The atmosphere of rumor and fear that prevailed during the months after the invasion favored extortion. Some Criollo landowners took advantage of the opportunity to threaten their Spanish counterparts with the destruction of their property if they did not pay large sums of money to the messengers delivering the threats. The connection between extortionists and the bands was never completely established in court.[27]

One of the most notorious extortion accusations made during this period was that of Antonio Javierre and Luis M. Marín, of Maricao, and Antonio Amill and Bartolo Almodóvar, of Sabana Grande, against Vicente Sulsona of Sabana Grande, and his associates Manuel Sulsona, Isidro Márquez and Pedro Beauchamp. According to Marín, around October 28, 1898, Manuel Sulsona appeared at his hacienda in Maricao with the following written message:

> Rio Prieto Headquarters
> According to what this council has agreed, you are to pay the amount of *one thousand* pesos as soon as possible, and if you refuse we will cut off your ears, hang you and burn your properties.
> Manuel J. Rodríguez
> Antonio Jero

Marín explained to Sulsona that he did not have a thousand pesos at the moment. Sulsona then asked him to sign a promissory note for 400 pesos, which Marín endorsed in the following manner:

> I have received from Playa Hermanos the amount of *four hundred* pesos cash in provincial money. Maricao, October 28, 1898.
> [signed] Luis M. Marín

The amount is $400.00

On October 30, Marín sent a note to Playa Hermanos, in Mayagüez:

On the 28th of this month, I issued in your name a receipt for $400 *four hundred* pesos. As things are so bad around here, even signatures are being forged, I ask that you do not issue any order for payment or draw any amount until you are notified.

However, Isidro Márquez, one of Sulsona's associates, had already drawn and cashed the amount from Playa Hermanos.[28]

Antonio Javierre, for his part, declared that around October 21, Pedro Beauchamp came to his farm and asked him to sign a document for 250 pesos in favor of Vicente Sulsona, Pedro Beauchamp and Isidro Márquez, to keep his farm from being burned down. Javierre signed the note but did not pay. Vicente Sulsona then called him to his Hacienda La Guaba in Maricao. Javierre agreed in the presence of Beauchamp, Márquez and Manuel Sulsona to pay the specified amount. He also owed Sulsona 68 pesos from previous transactions. The burning of several neighborhood haciendas greatly encouraged Javierre to agree to pay Sulsona.[29]

Assassination and Homicide

The number of assassinations and homicides related to the bands in Puerto Rico during 1898–99 is difficult to estimate. Statistics available for those years do not specify the circumstances of death. In any case, they refer to crimes settled in court, and were fewer in number than those resolved in most previous years.[30]

Some violent deaths that occurred during the months following the invasion are illustrative of their vindictive character.

On October 23, 1898, a band "came down firing on an hacienda house in Adjuntas, shooting and killing overseer Vicente Morey, and afterwards cutting his throat."[31]

Around ten thirty at night on October 28, some twenty men armed with machetes and firearms, blackened with charcoal and masked, entered the house of Criollo coffee grower Prudencio Méndez, in Barrio Algarrobo in Yauco. They demanded 10 thousand pesos from him. Méndez answered he did not have that amount. Then, Eugenio Rodríguez, who was pointing at Mendez' head with a revolver, shot him. Méndez fell dead, and several of the attackers cut up his corpse with their machetes. They tied up his two sons and ransacked the house. Nicolás Feliciano then ordered the widow, Prudencia Mattei, to shoot her husband's corpse once. She refused and was slapped. Her two daughters, 19 and 20 years old, were brought in and forced to dance around the corpse to the music of a harmonica found in the house. After three hours the attackers left, threatening to come back if they were accused.

Eventually, six of the attackers were identified and five were captured. Nicolás Feliciano, to whom other crimes were attributed, was never found. The other five, Eugenio Rodríguez, nicknamed "La Bruja," his brother Simeón Rodríguez, Carlos Pacheco, his brother Hermógenes, and Rosalí Santiago, were tried in Ponce in December 1899. They were sentenced to death by garrote. The sentence was later commuted to life in prison.[32]

Jacobo Córdova Chirino has told of the murder of Antonio Delgado and the rape of two women in his home in Barrio Guayo in Adjuntas, on September 30, 1898. The Ponce District Court found five men guilty, and sentenced them to death in June 1900. Governor Hunt commuted the death penalty of the youngest, 21-year-old Juan Torres Acevedo, but refused to suspend the execution of the others, which was carried out on June 3, 1902.[33]

Other murders were never brought to trial. On the night of December 1, 1898, a band "of about eighty men" showed up at Guillermo Rullán's farm in Utuado. They fired into the air and threatened to burn the house down if the occupants did not come out. Two guards, a farm worker, and overseer Jaime Sancho came out and the latter handed them the keys to the house. The assailants, blackened with charcoal, loaded coffee, clothes, and other products on mules they had brought with them. They took the overseer to the machinery house, tied a rope around his neck and hanged him. The perpetrators of this murder were never found.[34]

Who Killed Claudio Mora?

The death of Claudio Mora Ruiz, in January 1899, shook the people of Utuado violently, as he was the nephew of Asturian Benito Ruiz Quevedo, one of the city's prominent figures. Mora's corpse was found down a hill on the Caonillas road with several wounds, one of which had pierced his heart.[35]

The authorities questioned everybody who had had any conflict with Mora. The file they built up is eloquent testimony to the conflict-ridden character of Utuado society during the period of the coffee boom. Peregrín Negrón Álvarez, a merchant and farmer from Viví Abajo, stated that "around two or three years ago he had a disagreement or difference with Mora about some land. As a consequence he had suffered imprisonment for ten months and a day, the sentence set by the Mayagüez court, which he served in the Arecibo jail." Elías Negrón Álvarez said Mora had been married to his cousin Joaquina Ruiz Álvarez, and that "about a year ago, he had had legal problems with Mora over some family rights regarding Mora's wanting to take possession of some land that did not belong to him, matters which are still pending resolution in the Supreme Court." He denied that "when the Americans invaded this City . . . he took the above-mentioned don Claudio Mora prisoner."

José Liberato Díaz said that "around two years ago a trial was held before the Municipal Court . . . regarding the claim to a property, the court ruled against him, and he filed an appeal before the Court of First Instance in Arecibo, which revoked the previous ruling; but, after that he has maintained friendly relations with don Claudio Mora." However, Díaz went further:

> he asked the Judge if his arrest was due to having had legal problems with don Claudio Mora, [because] there were other people who had had them also, and they were don Benito Ruiz, don Luis Rigual, and don Antonio Montero, with whom Mora had personal differences some years before.

Gregorio Morales Ramos was also called to testify. He stated that "around three years before he had filed a law suit against him [Mora] over the ownership of a plot of land. The suit was won by the contestant and he was awarded what was due him." Ezequiel Colom Ricalda, a day laborer and *agregado* on Mora's farm in Caonillas Arriba from the middle of December, answered when questioned saying that it was "completely false that he had blocked [Mora's] entrance to the afore-mentioned farm."

They all had alibis. Even those who testified about the suspects allegedly had been busy at work or traveling to Ponce on the day Mora died. The questioning shows the insistence of the authorities, trying to destroy the suspects' alibis. But the witnesses were equally tenacious: "it is true," one of them stated on January 30, "and he remembers perfectly that on the 20th . . . he saw the [suspect] busy . . . from six o'clock in the morning until dark, carrying coffee from his house to don Juan Casellas' house." In view of the impossibility of gathering evidence, the Mayagüez Court provisionally dismissed the case on June 19.

The case was reopened in November, when a worker accused a landowner with a medium-sized hacienda and an ex-guard of being the perpetrators of Mora's murder. But, in the end, Mora's death was never explained satisfactorily.

The Reaction of the Hacienda Owners

If the robberies, the fires, and the violent deaths during 1898–99 were not always specifically punished by the court, the ruling classes eventually regrouped to defend their interests. Already, by August 31, 1898, a group of landowners had signed a manifesto in the Mayagüez newspaper *La Bruja*:

> The Civil Guard, say what you may, was our protection against the dozens of thieves and escapees from prison and jails, who usually took refuge in the countryside. Although it is true that members of this force were not selected as carefully as called for in this case, it

is no less true they saved us from many of the upsetting situations we
are now going through. . . .[36]

The bands had begun attacking Spaniards; however, for the bands the
distinction between Spanish and Criollo hacienda owners was already
beginning to fade. In any case, the state of rebellion in the countryside
jeopardized the harvest and new planting. Things had to return to the way
they were. The "revolution" had ended.

The hacienda owners sought to consolidate their control over the workers in different ways. One was to assume a new role of representative of
the law and order in the countryside. For example, on January 8, 1899,
Lieutenant Elliot, the commander in Las Marías informed Colonel Carr,
commander in Mayagüez that Pepe Rivera, the son of hacienda owner
Domingo Rivera, had been intimidating the workers. Pretending to act
with the authorization of the American military, Pepe had appeared at
Teresa Colón's hacienda with a police officer from Mayagüez. He had
taken several workers prisoner and had kept them at Hacienda Canales for
three days. One worker, Evaristo Quiñones, assured Elliot that Rivera had
threatened to kill him. They had tied him to a wall by his thumbs to make
him confess that he knew who had robbed Constantino Hermida's home.
Elliot also took statements from workers Sebastián Quiñones, Leonardo
Colón, and Juan Rivera, the latter having received several machete-cuts
from Pepe Rivera. Pepe was arrested and jailed in Mayagüez, but the
Mayagüez mayor intervened and obtained his freedom.[37]

On the other hand, some hacienda owners used military protection
against the bands to reassert their power over their workers. One court file
shows they were attempting to impose this practice again on the mountain. José Cuevas, a 17-year-old day laborer, had worked for several
months on Antonino García's hacienda, in Barrio Angeles in Utuado. On
Christmas Eve, 1898, he told his employer he wanted to return to his
family home in Lares. He asked to settle his accounts. After deducting
what Cuevas had bought at the hacienda store from his wages, there was
a balance in his favor of 6 reales, or 75 cents in provincial money. García
wanted to give him a voucher for that amount so that Cuevas could

recover it in goods at the Velilla Hermanos store in Lares. Cuevas insisted on being paid in cash. García refused and ordered his son Guillermo to prepare the voucher. According to Antonino García's statement,

> . . . Cuevas was hacking with a machete at the root of a flamboyan tree close to the house, and uttering threats. . . . García went down to the machinery house, and while he was busy covering a tray that collects water from the machine, Cuevas appeared at the door and threw a stone at him, hitting him on the left side of his body. He immediately threw himself upon Cuevas and grabbed his wrist, because he had a machete. Cuevas cut him on the head. During the fight they both fell to the ground, because the floor was wet, and when they did Cuevas got up and ran, . . . followed by two Americans who are doing service in his [García's] home, and by his son Guillermo, but they could not catch him.[38]

This complaint differed in two important aspects from the report don Antonino had originally made. In the first one he alleged Cuevas "threw himself upon me with a machete to kill me," and "what happened was seen by two Americans who are staying in my home."[39]

One reason for García's modification of his original report may have been that he could not get the support of the two American soldiers guarding his farm. When the incident occurred, one of the soldiers was "at the back of the stable eating oranges." The second one, John Vandergreff, said he did not see the incident because he had gone inside the house minutes earlier. He saw only the wounds García showed him and Cuevas running off "with some kind of metal object" until he disappeared into the coffee bushes.

It is worth noting how old hacienda owner García, backed by two armed soldiers, tried to impose his order and working conditions. It is also interesting that day laborer Cuevas questioned and resisted the arbitrary way in which he was denied even the right to use freely the meager remnant of his wages, after working for several months.

The lack of cash, added to the difficulty of getting financing, led the hacienda owners to attempt to return to the old system of paying wages with vouchers and tokens. The workers resisted this type of compensation because vouchers were only redeemable in overpriced goods at hacienda stores. This situation caused several strikes during the sugar cane harvest of 1899. In Fajardo, Commander General Grant, of the northern military district, mediated and imposed the Solomonic solution that wages be paid half in cash and half in vouchers.[40]

Military measures did not always favor the hacienda owners' interests. Military Governor Henry, for example, tried to impose an eight-hour workday. The hacienda owners protested furiously. In Manatí, hacienda owner Francisco Calaf preferred to stop the harvest rather than to implement Henry's order. According to Calaf, the measure would cause him to lose around 200 dollars a day.[41] After Davis replaced Henry—which *La Democracia* considered a victory for Muñoz Rivera and his followers in Washington—the 8-hour workday in the agricultural sector vanished.

In 1899, several landowners in the Ponce municipal area contracted Ramón Morell Campos to carry out "a campaign to promulgate morality throughout the jurisdiction," from March to May. According to Morell's report to the municipal government, his work served to get people back on the path of peace and order, "in contrast to the violent social and economic unrest that had developed, and which led honest working people down a dangerous slope." For his mission he relied on the help of ward stewards, rural teachers, and "well-established landowners":

> With such good people at my side, we have defended Property and harmonized the interests of both property and labor, always within the law presently in force. We have explained doctrines of law and order and moral precepts, helping considerably in the administration of justice in its noble mission. We have explained their duties and rights to all citizens. In summary, this mission has not created any political friction . . . for which reason the campaign has been very broad and well respected. With no fear whatsoever, I have taken it to the most remote villages and places, where ill-advised people might preach crime or any other dissolute idea.[42]

The measures taken by the military regime to help the dispossessed after Hurricane San Ciriaco (August 8, 1899) strengthened the hacienda owner's hand. With the support of Davis' military government, by September 1899, the landowners had managed to reestablish their hegemony, and law and order, in most of the Puerto Rican countryside. There were still occasional nocturnal bands, but the uprising in the countryside had come to an end.

Public Opinion and the Bands

Since August 1898, the Puerto Rico press had been debating the impact of the bands in the mountains. The conservative press denounced the attacks on Spanish persons and property, but newspapers established in Puerto Rico after the invasion went as far as to question the existence of the bands themselves. For example, *La Estrella Solitaria*, published in Ponce, protested on October 4, 1898:

> *La Correspondencia de Puerto Rico* is a newspaper which is totally sympathetic to Spain and, to add insult to injury, a defender of the clergy. Its eagerness to present the people of this country as disruptive of law and order is unbridled. News about fires and armed robberies, almost always carried out according to *"tía Javiera"* on the farms of Spaniards, constantly appear in its columns. . . . It is time for the press in this country to be more serious in its reporting.
>
> We vigorously protest against those publications that feed on false news only, attempting to sow panic in the Puerto Rican community.
>
> To be or not to be.[43]

However, *La Estrella Solitaria* could not deny the obvious. *El País*, which even before Brooke took charge had proclaimed itself sympathetic to the new regime, voiced its regret on October 15, 1898, regarding the bands:

> There are regions which have suffered as many as seventeen farm burnings; in others, attacks on people have become as frequent. This is new in Puerto Rico, and it seems as if the devil has unleashed his forces against us to make us lose our way and to discredit us.

> Yesterday, General Brooke was telling two friends of ours: I am very upset because I see people confuse freedom with license. They must be educated and I urge you to begin this regenerating task, firmly and with perseverance. . . .
>
> At this critical moment, the people of the United States are observing and studying us to conclude if we deserve all the rights that are the basis of their great progress.[44]

However, judging by the United States press, the American people had their eyes on the signs of rebellion from the Philippines and the strained relationships between Cuba and the United States, rather than on the bands of *tiznados* in Puerto Rico. It was not until almost the middle of November that some American newspapers began to pay attention to the level of violence occurring at the Puerto Rican countryside. This attention was due in part to Puerto Rican businessmen repeatedly petitioning their agents in the United States to air the matter in the press. This was one way of pressuring the military to act. The specific petition that triggered the issue was that the merchants and hacienda owners of San Sebastián insisted that a military detail be posted there. Brooke had arranged for soldiers to be stationed in Aguadilla and Lares to patrol the district, but San Sebastián's leading sectors considered this insufficient protection.

On November 18, 1898, the assistant adjutant general of the Army in Washington instructed Brooke to investigate a report from "a trustworthy New York firm" regarding disturbances and depredations in Puerto Rico, particularly in San Sebastián. The firm in question was Frank, Halberstad & Co., and its correspondent was Santisteban, Chavarri and Co., of San Juan. On November 22, the assistant adjutant general sent a request to Brooke from President McKinley to investigate the plunderings committed in Yauco. The Lanman and Kemp Company of New York had reported them. On the 25th, the assistant sent Brooke a communication from the president, and a letter from L. W. & P. Armstrong of New York, quoting a Ponce firm which complained of having to suspend business due to the violence occurring at the countryside. On the 26th, the assistant adjutant general again communicated by cable reporting that the New York firms continued to receive complaints of disturbances in Yauco, Adjuntas,

Comerío, Barros and Las Marías "that large bodies of armed men are overrunning the country, setting fire to property and murdering people."[45]

The military government in Puerto Rico firmly denied that disturbances were continuing. On November 21, Brooke answered the War Department that the bands were a thing of the past and that for the last three or four weeks everything had been peaceful, thanks to intensive patrolling. Brooke alleged that reports had been exaggerated.[46]

The American press spread Brooke's statement, managing to silence public opinion. However, Washington continued to supervise the Puerto Rico military government in regard to public order. On December 8, General Henry, Brooke's successor, reacted with exasperation to the communications of the assistant adjutant general:

> Our troops are centrally located and patrol the country constantly, and if they only give us the information troops move at once to arrest these bandits, but so far I have been unable to get information from these people. . . . If the orderly class referred to in this letter will help me by giving the information, which they doubtless possess, disorder will cease, but from my experience in the island statements by the people or articles in newspapers are to be received with a great deal of allowance and particularly so in the face of constant patrols and reports of intelligent and reliable Army Officers, who should know the facts better than citizens who are not here on the spot.[47]

The Bands and the Political Parties

The Criollos' reluctance to denounce the participants in the acts of outrage and vengeance occurring at the countryside led the American military to believe that there was a connection between the political parties and the *tiznados*. On December 18, for example, Brigadier General Grant relayed the opinion of the military commander of Arecibo to the assistant adjutant general of the Puerto Rico Military Department. The commander in Arecibo believed it was appropriate to integrate pure Orthodox Party members into the Arecibo municipal government, which was in the hands of the *Muñocistas*, or liberal Autonomists: "From all that I can learn the

Orthodox party having no representation are not sorry to see disturbances continue, and in fact, if they do not actually encourage the disorders they make no effort to stop them and are secretly glad that they continue as this is the only hope they have of getting into power."[48]

The military suspected that some municipal officials were covering up for those responsible for the bands. On November 2, for example, General Grant sent the military governor a report from Colonel Tyson saying that the mayor from Hatillo was "connected with the bandits." On December 18, Grant repeated the accusation and requested an investigation of the mayor and the municipal government of Hatillo. Grant returned to the attack on January 25, charging with corruption "the whole municipal government of Hatillo." In particular, he accused the secretary of the Municipal Court of extortion.[49]

In fact, some military men came to believe there was a connection between the bands and the liberal Autonomists. By the middle of December 1898, commanders of various military posts in Puerto Rico and Vieques were alerted to possible disturbances and rebellious events during the Christmas season, especially around New Year's. For this reason the commanding officer of Toa Alta asked if they were going to authorize the celebration of the midnight mass on Christmas. The assistant to the commander in Mayagüez cabled the commander at Aguadilla saying they were expecting "an uprising of the people in the mountains." Brigadier General Grant ordered his subordinates to intensify their patrolling before January 1. Christmas, however, was rather peaceful in most parts of the island. This signified a truce in the operations of the bands.[50]

CHAPTER FIVE

The American Military and the Bands

During the weeks following the invasion, the high military command became aware that collective acts of retaliation were being perpetrated against the Spanish hacienda owners and merchants on the island. Some were carried out under the pretext of collaborating with the invading forces. After the armistice, the American military authorities began to grow alarmed at the demonstrations of revenge against Spaniards. When the newspaper *La Estrella Solitaria* called for revenge for the deaths in Ciales on August 13, General Gilmore closed down the newspaper and sent its editor Luis Cavalier to prison.[1] Wilson tried to act equally severely toward the perpetrators of a fire in Barrio Coto, on the night of August 18, but the military commission called for that purpose could not establish who was finally responsible for the act.

In the transition period between August and October, army patrols attended to the lack of safety on the roads. In the occupied zone, many hacienda owners requested that the district commanders post soldiers at night in pairs to protect their properties.[2] This way, the military tasks of protection and patrol brought on the first confrontations between the military and the bands.

The Tiznados as Bandits

During confrontations, band members were treated as "bandits," according to the Far West model imported by the Americans.[3] The elements of pillage and vengeance of the bands overshadowed their claim for social justice. The American press, in its relatively scarce coverage of the bands, characterized the rebels as bandits.[4] The new rulers, abstracting from the economic crisis, the hunger, the abject poverty, and the previous history of social conflict in the mountainous areas, defined the problem as one of law and order. In light of this definition, they understood their task to be the eradication of the criminals who threatened public peace.

Difficulties with the District Courts: Utuado

Very soon the military discovered that Puerto Rico's court proceedings and principles were different from those of the American army. For example, ex-convict Adolfo Amato had been accused by an Arecibo rural merchant of being the leader of a band in his neighborhood and of extortion. Amato was arrested and sentenced by the Arecibo court. Major Charles K. Darling, of the Massachusetts' 6th Regiment of Volunteers, recommended to Colonel Tyson, then the military commander of Arecibo, that he publicly execute Amato immediately, as a means of restoring peace in the district. Even though Tyson supported Darling's recommendation, General Brooke rejected it. Eventually, Amato was tried and acquitted by a military tribunal.[5]

On December 7, the assistant to the general commander in Mayagüez sent a strong reprimand to his subordinate, Lieutenant A.H. Elliott, of the 5th Cavalry, then commander at Las Marías:

> I am directed by the Commanding Officer to inform you that it was reported to him this morning by a reliable party that you had advised or suggested to the Chief of Police of Las Marías that he should shoot or inflict other summary punishment on four prisoners, robbers, or incendiaries, already in custody of the police. This report seems incredible, and this letter is written to ask you if it is true or not; and to advise you to be careful to make no remarks that may be misconstrued and give rise to such reports.[6]

Above all, the military was surprised at the slowness of the proceedings, and by the prosecutors' difficulty in gathering evidence against those accused of participating in the bands.

In September and October 1898, the Utuado District Court declared itself unqualified to take action on the accusations and reports of robberies and fires on the haciendas. Technically, the state of war continued, and thus the reported crimes fell under military jurisdiction. Since most part of the Utuado court district was in the American zone, Judge Félix Santoni transferred the case files to the Ponce military command.

In the first week of November, the cases were returned from Ponce with instructions to try them in the civil courts. By then, the number of unresolved cases had markedly increased and the District Attorney's office did not have the human or material resources to face the avalanche of paper coming down on it. As the number of accused increased due to the inability of the courts to speed up the charging of prisoners, jails became overcrowded. On the other hand, the reluctance of witnesses to give statements made resolution of the charges impossible.

Public opinion was divided. Some people pressured the authorities to end the bands' nocturnal activities, extortion, and stealing. Others constantly demanded that the accused be freed, and that more convincing evidence be required to prosecute them. Under these circumstances, it is not surprising that the military thought the Criollo judges and prosecutors lacked the will to try those guilty of the homicides, fires, and robberies committed in the countryside after the invasion.

Responding to this frame of mind, Governor Henry decided in December to assign some band-related cases to military commissions in San Juan, Ponce, and Mayagüez.[7] In February, he created a commission in Arecibo. The military commission was a kind of court-martial for civilians in territories where a state of war prevailed. As the United States Senate had not yet ratified the Treaty of Paris, the state of war technically continued. Protected by this, Henry appointed military subordinates to try Criollos accused of homicides, fires, and armed robberies. The commissions in San Juan, Arecibo, Mayagüez, and Ponce were in session from January to April 1899. The San Juan commission only tried one band case, that of Juan Valle Mojica, a shoemaker from Cidra accused and convicted of assault and robbery in Aguas Buenas.[8] The Arecibo commission tried a few cases, each one consisting of several defendants. The Mayagüez and Ponce commissions tried the most important cases.

The Form of the Military Commissions

Each court consisted of three army officers who acted as judges and one judge-advocate who acted as prosecutor. In at least one case the prosecutor acted as defense attorney, too. These panels also acted as courts-martial to try cases of insubordination among the troops. The civilians accused could bring civilian attorneys to defend them before the military commissions. In addition, they could represent themselves or request the court to appoint officers as their defense attorneys. The court provided for an interpreter and secretarial staff to transcribe interrogatories and results of deliberations.

Although in appearance this format guaranteed the defendant an impartial trial, military judges usually lacked adequate legal training to adjudicate cases fairly and impartially. The appointment of an interpreter did not necessarily guarantee adequate translation of witnesses' testimony and the defense's arguments. Civilian attorneys, used to Puerto Rico court procedures and formalisms, considered the decisions of military judges too peremptory and brusque. The format of the military commission imitated the haste of the military courts. Cases that would have taken a much longer time in a civil court were dealt with in one or two sessions. With this time pressure, there was no way final legal pleas—written and translated into English—could even summarize the essential elements of the defense.

In these circumstances, it is surprising that military commissions acquitted 40 percent of defendants accused of participating in the bands.

Military Commissions and Public Opinion

The angry protests of Juan González Font and other defense attorneys against decisions by the military judges disposed public opinion against the military commissions. Once the United States Senate ratified the Treaty of Paris, there was no justification for trying some Puerto Ricans in military courts. Some writers proposed in the newspapers that defendants, both in military and civilian courts, be granted amnesty, as they had committed criminal acts under passions aroused by the sudden political change.

Table 5.1
Persons Accused of Participating in the Bands and Tried Before Military Commissions in 1899

	Accused	Acquitted
Arecibo	11	5
Mayagüez	14	5
Ponce	26	11
San Juan	1	0
Total	**52**	**21**

Source: Special Orders and case files in RG 153.

The military judges could not understand the history of conflict that had preceded the outbreak of the bands. They missed the subtleties in the legal arguments of the Puerto Rican lawyers. Sentences were too severe. Thus, a general pardon should be decreed.

In September 1899, Juan Torreforte wrote:

Most are hard-working men, useful citizens, faithful Puerto Ricans. If they committed offenses, they were driven by the patriotic enthu-siasm that overtook these noble people when, by American initiative, the abominable tyranny of Spain was overthrown. During those important days, the people of this country opened their hearts to the best of hopes. The souls of these poor prisoners were filled with wild enthusiasm and drunk with joy. These feelings rise with inexpressable rapture in the heart of a patriot who, having been a slave all his life, sees the shackles that bind him broken in one glorious instant. . . .

. . . All was the immediate consequence of that state of affairs. All this is logical and explainable in a society that violently passes from a power that has oppressed her to another that offers to redeem her.[9]

The military was not exempt from the pressure created by the opinion held by the Criollos. Henry himself wanted to dramatize the impartiality and purity of the military court procedures.[10] However, in the end it was impossible to continue with procedures foreign to Puerto Rico.

Main Difficulties

The Mayagüez and Ponce military commissions tried the most notorious cases. In Mayagüez, several of the accused were relatives of prominent families in the area. In Ponce, one of the most important cases was the burning of Arbona's store in Barrio Guaraguao and the threats to his neighbors. Although the ties with the leading Criollo sectors were not as obvious, the case concerned a neighborhood leader from the Autonomist Party and his relatives.

The flowery oratory and dramatic gestures of attorney González Font provoked an unfavorable reaction among Ponce's military judges. In their court-room experience, they had no language but the plain statement of the facts. Something similar happened in Mayagüez with the rhetorical efforts of Criollo attorney William Bryan.

In Mayagüez and Ponce, the interpreters' mistakes caused both anger and hilarity. The military did not give too much credence to the alibis presented by family and friends of the accused. Following is one of the questionings that typified the two mentalities, when Victorio Rivera, a 14-year-old witness for the defense, faced one judge's questions:

Q. Can you read and write?
A. No, sir.
Q. Have you been to school?
A. No, sir.
Q. Have you ever been to church?
A. No, sir.[11]

The judge's own questions thus called the credibility of this witness into question. The judges had no patience either with the subtleties of the defense's cross-examinations. Governor Henry rapidly confirmed the rulings of the military commissions, without benefit of any appeal.

The Defendants

Between February and April 1899, the military commissions tried 70 men, but only accused 52 of committing crimes related to the bands. Among the rest there were civilians attached to the army tried for negligence or infractions in the execution of duty. There were also Criollos accused of fighting with military men, or of some petty theft or transgression connected with military property. Civilian Rafael Ortiz was accused and found guilty of killing a soldier in Caguas for personal reasons.[12]

The men tried for being members of the bands were almost all accused of committing violent acts or extortion. Most lived in the central-western part of the island, were 20 to 30 years old, and were owners or relatives of owners of small farms, or day laborers. Their victims usually were farmers and merchants.

Those found guilty of participating in the bands were given sentences of 2 to 12 years in prison at hard labor. Some were pardoned at the end of several years in jail, but most served their terms with the appropriate reductions for good behavior. At least one died in prison before serving his full sentence; most returned to the municipalities where they had previously lived.

The contemporary press never treated these people as heroes. Once they were found guilty, the main defense offered them was that they were victims of their passions or naive followers of vengeful elements.

"White Eagle's Band of Outlaws"

White Eagle

Of all the figures related to the band's activities at that time, José Maldonado, or "White Eagle," made the deepest impression on collective memory. As usually happens with this type of character, tradition has preserved only the hazy traits of his life and has idealized his acts.[13]

Before the invasion, José Maldonado was the most notorious figure in a group of youngsters accused of several robberies and acts of aggression. He was born in Juana Díaz between 1872 and 1874 and was a barber by profession. His nicknames before 1898 seem to have been "Black Eagle" and "Blue Eagle." His sphere of activity centered on the municipalities of Juana Díaz and Ponce.

According to a penal file summarized in *La Democracia*, José Maldonado served a jail sentence for stealing from June 19, 1887, to January 19, 1889. On April 1, 1890, he was jailed for wounding someone and was released on March 20, 1891. On February 7 of the same year "he began serving a sentence for an attempted murder, and was pardoned on November 30, 1892." He was in jail from September 28 to October 3, 1893, accused of stealing. He was again jailed from March 2, 1894, to February 7, 1895, for the same crime. On March 3 of that year, he went to prison again for wounding someone and was pardoned on June 22. On October 25, 1895, was accused of fraud, was released on November 2, and was returned to jail for the same crime on March 13, 1896. He was freed on May 26. He went back to prison for attempted murder on March 21, 1898, and escaped. He left for New York and returned after the invasion.[14]

The earliest mention in the consulted American military documents of someone who could be White Eagle is dated August 16, 1898. On that date, General Henry, then living in Utuado, told Gilmore, Miles' Assistant Adjutant General, that there was "a band of bandits or banditti" in Jayuya. He added that their leader The Eagle had warned the bandits about American cavalry sent to chase them.[15]

The next time the military letters mention White Eagle is on December 18. On that date, Juana Díaz telegraph operator Bell informed headquarters in San Juan that "White Eagle and his band of 17 outlaws were seen in town on the 17th." They were blamed for the burning of a plantation located one mile west of town. On the 19th, Colonel Burke reported his efforts to capture the bandits, but he thought While Eagle was in San Juan.[16]

Between December 26 and 28, 1898, *El Correo de Puerto Rico* published a letter from José Maldonado, "White Eagle," addressed to newspaper director Eugenio Deschamps. Probably, Deschamps touched up or even drafted what Maldonado told him. In the letter, Maldonado told in detail why he had been in conflict with the Spanish police from the time he was eleven years old. He said, "This is the story of my life I wish you would print in your newspaper, having been the victim of much abuse and many injustices." According to Maldonado, his difficulties with the Spanish police arose because of his refusal to become a spy, an informant and a hired killer.

. . . once, they managed to surround me in a sugarcane field in the jurisdiction of Juana Díaz, but they did not dare come in, nor could I come out or eat without the risk of being captured. After three days of hunger, I decided to come out. A fight developed between us that ended with their running away after I wounded one of them. In those days some kind-hearted gentlemen gave me 300 pesos that I spent on clothes. I entrusted them to a black man called Emilio, but he handed them to the Chief of Police, leaving me naked. I chased him, and when I found him at the corner of Union and Vives Streets, I shot him twice and left him for dead. The police then began firing at me. . . . I fled to the country . . . where I was surprised by . . . two pairs [of soldiers], who shot at me. I defended myself with two revolvers, wounding one soldier and making the other one flee. A few days later, Don Abelardo Moscoso, who was being followed and whom . . . they tried to kill, was preparing to leave. I went to him and begged him to take me with him. We both left on a ship for New York. There I went to the Cuban Embassy and was sent to Cuba with an expedition. Declaring myself an American citizen, I returned wounded to New York; there I waited to go back with the expedition that was to attack Puerto Rico.

At last I returned to my country wishing to live peacefully near my mother and brothers and sisters, and, as I am only 24 years old, to work honestly and be useful to society. However, just as if we were in the times of the Spaniards, a sharp tongue has turned the American leaders against me, and they are pursuing me to kill me.

In view of this, I've gone to the mountains with a band, and I am ready to punish all Spaniards, without harming Americans.

But I still restrain myself somewhat, to see if I may be pardoned, as I have not committed any crime. But if I am not pardoned, I will not be responsible for the consequences.[17]

Through Deschamps, the pardon was granted in January.[18]

In May 1899, José Maldonado was involved in a confrontation with the Ponce police which arose from an incident while in line for a smallpox vaccination. He was later arrested at his home. In an effort to rescue him, his band was involved in a shoot-out right in the center of Ponce. Two of Maldonado's followers were fatally shot, and White Eagle himself lost an eye. *El Combate*, a newspaper belonging to Evaristo Izcoa Díaz, demanded his freedom ("a poor wretch who is more decent and honorable than many judges"). However, other newspapers supported the municipal authorities on the charging and imprisonment of Maldonado, who was accused of extortion. None of the newspapers, in favor or against, attributed a political ideology to him.[19]

For the Americans, "White Eagle" became a synonym for bandit, and the bands' actions were generally attributed to him. In 1899, the editor of *Our Islands and Their People* published a photograph, probably from the days of the invasion, of a group of Puerto Ricans with a one-star flag, and entitled it "White Eagle's Band of Outlaws."[20] This photograph, published again in recent years, has caused some to believe that José Maldonado, "White Eagle," organized a band to resist the American invasion.

CHAPTER SIX

The Military and Puerto Rico

The volunteer troops from Wisconsin, Illinois, Ohio, Pennsylvania and Massachusetts that had taken part in the invasion began returning to the United States at the end of August 1898. Most troops that replaced the volunteers consisted of regular soldiers. The 47th Regiment of Volunteers from New York, which served in Puerto Rico from October 1898 to April 1899, was one of the exceptions. The 1st Cavalry Regiment of Volunteers from Kentucky also served around three months at the end of 1898.

Among the professional soldiers who arrived during the last months of 1898 to replace the volunteers, the 5th Cavalry Regiment is noteworthy. This unit, General Henry's favorite, had been tempered in the American West on campaigns against the Indians, mostly the Sioux. Most of the officers of the 5th Cavalry were career soldiers.[1]

The 5th Cavalry took on most of the patrolling against the seditious bands. Because of their experience against the Sioux, they were sent to the municipalities most affected by the bands. Their colonel assumed military command of Mayagüez. The regiment's mobility compensated for the small number of members.

Two regular infantry regiments, the 11th and the 19th, were stationed in San Juan, Ponce and along the coast, and on the eastern side of the island. Frank McIntyre, from Alabama, was one of the officers of the 19th Regiment, but Henry made him his assistant in his administration. Years later, McIntyre directed Puerto Rico's affairs in the Bureau of Insular Affairs of the War Department in Washington.[2]

In general, the professional infantry regiments had less contact with the activities of the *tiznados* than the cavalry did. However, they dealt with the civilian population in the course of other duties and investigations. The 47th Regiment of Volunteers from New York was active in the region of Caguas. There, the Irish soldiers drank, danced, loved and fought to such a degree as to worry the high command in San Juan. The short time the Kentucky cavalry was active on the island was dedicated to patrolling the mountainous areas, especially Ciales and Las Marías.

Profile of the Officers in the Area of the Bands

Twenty officers appear most active in the area of the bands during 1898–99. Of these, eight belonged to the 5th Cavalry Regiment and the rest to the 6th, 11th, and 19th Regular Infantry. A collective profile of the twenty officers* may provide interesting material for thought: Of the twenty, two were European (one German and one Hungarian), five were from the Northeast of the United States, four from the Middle West, one from the West, six from the South, and two whose birthplaces are unknown. At least eleven of the eighteen had studied in military academies. Four had enlisted in the army during the Civil War and had subsequently received commissions as regular officers.[3]

These officers, of different ages and backgrounds, showed different attitudes in their relationships with Puerto Ricans. There was no uniform behavior or model of thought. For example, for Captain Seaborn G. Chiles of the 11th Infantry, "a more helpless and worthless set of people it is hard to imagine. In my opinion they are far inferior to our southern negroes, and but little if any better than our Indians. They certainly have all their vices with none of their virtues."[4] On the other hand, Captains Macomb in Arecibo and Vernou in Yauco were greatly interested in civic projects. Captain Mansfield, Chiles' predecessor in Aguadilla, seemed attracted by economic matters. In Aibonito, Wheeler's interest in matters related to health, his field of specialty, was notable.

*See Table 6.1, pp. 100–101.

The American Says . . .

Officers communicated with most Puerto Ricans through interpreters. It is fascinating to see the development of the exchanges between the invaders and the invaded through third persons. At first, the military depended on Cubans who came with the troops, and on Americans and Europeans who knew some Spanish. For example, convict Adolphus Leslie was brought out of prison in Ponce to serve as interpreter in August 1898.[5] In October and November of the same year, James Jafetson, a native of Saint Thomas, served as an interpreter for the commander at Maricao in exchange for food and small gifts.[6] Eventually, they began hiring Puerto Ricans who had lived in the United States.

The task of these people was much more than translating the meanings of words. It was also necessary to interpret the respective ways of seeing things, which during the first weeks after the invasion were mutually foreign, and sometimes even disconcerting.

It is not surprising that some interpreters profited from their advantageous situation, while others were the easy target of groundless suspicions and distrust. On August 21, Miles ordered the arrest of an interpreter who had accompanied the troops to Barrio Coto on the morning after a fire, and who was accused of committing an unspecified crime. On August 28, Antonio Orta, from Barrio Bateyes, denounced to the commander at Mayagüez the outrage he had suffered in his home at the hands of a drunken interpreter. The interpreter, called Pedro, had put a gun to his chest. On December 1898, the assistant to the Adjutant General of the San Juan military district wrote to the commander in Barceloneta saying he had received bad reports about the interpreter who worked there. He said, "The interpreters must be upstanding men, and I understand that some of them are charging natives for interpreting their wants to our officials." On December 28, Brigadier General Grant asked the commander in Vieques to arrest and send to San Juan one Pepe Renaoz, if he was working as an interpreter there.[7]

In December, the mayor also accused some Majorcans in Maricao of creating a disturbance by blowing a bugle and yelling, "Long live Spain!"

TABLE 6.1

**American Officers Active in the Zone of the Seditious Bands,
1898–99**

Name	Place of Birth	Military Academy	Officer's Commission
Cornelius C.C. Carr	Virginia		1862
Seaborn Chiles			
Stephen H. Elliott	Georgia	1882	1886
Woodbridge Geary	Oregon d. Philippines	1878	1882
Henry J. Goldman	New York	1873	1877
Alonzo Gray	Wisconsin	1883	1887
Odon Gurovits	Hungary		1886
Christian C. Hewitt	Virginia	1870	1874
John M. Jenkins	South Carolina	1883	1887
Samuel G. Jones	Alabama	1886	1890
Harry R. Lee	Rhode Island	1885	1889
Francis W. Mansfield	Ohio	1866	1871
Alex McGuard	Illinois	1866	1871
Augustus C. Macomb	Michigan		1878
Albert L. Myer	New York	Private 1865	1867
Isaac de Russy	Virginia	Private 1861	
Charles A. Vernou	Pennsylvania	Private 1862	
C.W. Wadsworth			
Charles Watts	New York	1868	1872
Homer W. Wheeler	Vermont	Private 1875	

Comdr.: Military Post Commander

Mil. Comm.: Military Commission

Rank	Position
Col. 5th Cav.	Comdr. in Mayagüez; Judge in Mayagüez Mil. Comm.
Lt. 11th Inf.	Comdr. in Aguadilla 1899
1st Lt. 5th Cav.	Comdr. in Las Marías 1898
1st. Lt. 19th Inf.	Stationed in Yauco
1st Lt. 5th Cav.	
1st Lt. 5th Cav.	Comdr. in San Germán; Judge in Arecibo Mil. Comm.
1st Lt. 11th Inf.	Judge Advocate in Mayagüez Mil. Comm.
Capt. 19th Inf.	Judge in Ponce and Arecibo Mil. Comm.
1st Lt. 5th Cav.	Assistant to the Comdr. in Mayagüez
2nd Lt. 5th Cav.	Judge Advocate in Arecibo Mil. Comm.
	Comdr. in Lares
Capt. 11th Inf.	Comdr. in Aguadilla in 1898–99
Capt. 19th Inf.	
Capt. 5th Cav.	Comdr. in Arecibo; Judge in Arecibo Mil. Comm.
Capt. 11th Inf.	Comdr. in Ponce; Judge in San Juan Mil. Comm.
Col. 11th Inf.	Comdr. in Mayagüez 1898
Capt. 9th Inf.	Comdr. in Yauco; Judge in Ponce Mil. Comm.
Capt. 6th Inf.	Comdr. in Lares 1898
Capt. 5th Cav.	Comdr. in Adjuntas
Capt. 5th Cav.	Comdr. in Aibonito

Sources: Official Army Register 1897, and military correspondence of 1898–99 in RG 395.

A neighbor from Las Marías wrote to warn the mayor of Mayagüez that the Las Marías interpreter was going to intercede for the Maricao Majorcans:

> This interpreter (who says he is Cuban and a rebel in Cuba) has done his best to defend anything that seems Spanish. Public opinion has it that Spaniards in this jurisdiction and in Maricao subsidize him (or rather, "they have bought him off") to stay here and help them. This is terrible for us. A false Cuban, a false enemy of the Spaniards, is playing us into their [the Majorcans'] hands just by knowing English, and by influencing the American officer who has him in his service.[8]

Initially, interpreters charged up to 60 dollars a month, but when there were enough applicants for employment, they were paid even less than mule drivers. Around the end of 1898, Lieutenant Wright, commander in Guánica, requested the services of an interpreter from his superior in Yauco in the following terms:

> It is not possible for me to purchase fresh beef and fuel without the aid of an interpreter, or if there is disorder of any kind, with an interpreter it can be more easily investigated. One can be hired for about fifteen dollars per month.[9]

Captain Vernou in Yauco endorsed the request, as long as they could get the services for ten dollars a month.

The Americans trusted interpreters who spoke good English more, even if they could not be sure of their knowledge of Spanish. Ernest Jaencke, for example, was the interpreter in several trials for the Ponce military commission. Doubts about the accuracy of the translation of the testimony may be perceived in the following exchange, at Pedro Vargas' trial:

> Q. Do you live near the store of Arbona that was burned?
> A. I live at a short distance.
> Q. What do you call "retirado"?
> A. About one league.

In spite of such clear indications of deficiency, the Judge Advocate insisted on and managed to have Jaencke serve as interpreter in the case of Bautista González, which followed.[10]

Privates had to get their own interpreters to relate to civilians, and they frequently used children:

> Children would walk along the street and hold up an article, saying the word in Spanish until you repeated the name of the article in English. Then they would go on their way repeating the English word aloud over and over until they claimed it as part of their new vocabulary.[11]

Soldiers and Civilians

The warm reception that the civilians gave the invading troops in Ponce, Yauco, San Germán, Utuado, Mayagüez, and other municipalities lent a special quality to the American volunteers' stay in Puerto Rico. Statements made by the volunteers on their return to the United States are evidence of the friendly relationships they developed with Puerto Rican civilians.[12]

The experience of the regular and volunteer troops that replaced the regiments from Illinois, Wisconsin, Ohio, Massachusetts and Pennsylvania, starting on September 1898, was very different. In some parts of the island the relation between the military and the civilians went through a difficult period of adjustment. For example, it is possible to note the deterioration of relations in Ponce and Mayagüez by the number of disciplinary actions taken against soldiers who had insulted or injured civilians.[13]

Initially, civilians hesitated to complain to the military authorities about the injuries caused by drunken and undisciplined soldiers.[14] However, due to the frequency of the incidents and the nature of the damage, the Ponce press soon informed the military authorities of the abuses being committed. Several civilians found out which military officers were responsible for ensuring the soldiers' good behavior toward the civilians and called them to report incidents of disturbances. The municipal authorities, egged

Portion of the 16th Regiment, Pennsylvania Volunteers

on by the citizens, began claiming greater assurances as to public order. For example, on August 29, 1898, Mayagüez Mayor Santiago Palmer, sent to the military commander of the city a report from the chief of the Fire Department regarding a serious disturbance:

> because a large number of American soldiers, completely drunk, were all over the streets of the town, it was in complete disorder, and it was necessary to ask headquarters for help and request that they send pairs of soldiers to pick up the drunks. . . .[15]

However, on some occasions the Puerto Rican civilians came to blows with the soldiers in resisting abuse. A notorious incident took place in the poor Cuba sector of Utuado, in January 1899. After a chain of incidents related to the entertainment that the soldiers sought in Cuba, one night a group of residents received the soldiers with a hail of stones. The commotion that followed may have caused Governor Henry's subsequent removal of the Utuado military detachment and the dismissal of Mayor Ramiro Martínez.[16]

Conflicts between civilians and soldiers were frequent in Ponce because large troop contingents were camped on its outskirts. At night, soldiers visited the bars and houses of prostitution in the city. The municipal authorities appealed frequently to the military commander. Some journalists insistently requested that soldiers be prohibited from being on the streets after eight o'clock at night.[17] Of course, business owners who benefited from the recreational habits of the soldiers did not support those measures.

However, the most serious confrontations between soldiers and civilians took place in Caguas. The lack of discipline among the New York volunteers stationed there may have exceeded the tolerance of the people of Caguas for their Bohemian conduct by far. However, it may be also that there were many cigar-makers and hand-laborers in the urban area of Caguas, and this counterbalanced and challenged the New York soldiers. The pitched battles between civilians and soldiers on the streets of Caguas caught the attention of the authorities. Finally, a brawl between soldier John Burke of Brooklyn and hand-laborer Rafael Ortiz, apparently over a woman's favors, shook everyone. It ended with the soldier's death.[18] Shortly afterwards, the 47th Regiment returned to New York and was not replaced.

The reasons for the clashes between soldiers and civilians during 1898–99 ranged from the most trivial to the most sublime. For example, the impossibility of communicating in words could make people sometimes settle misunderstandings, often under the influence of alcohol, with fistfights and stabbings. On Christmas eve 1898, a row occurred between municipal policemen and soldiers in Las Marías. Three drunken soldiers started arguing with two policemen at eleven o'clock at night. Lack of knowledge of both languages intensified the conflict. According to Police Officer Práxedes Basora, the only thing he understood was a phrase the soldiers repeated: "Sons of bitches." In the fight that followed, Police Officer Basora hit one of the soldiers with a billy club, and a soldier shot and killed the other policeman.[19]

The indiscriminate use of firearms by soldiers caused numerous incidents, some of them fatal. At Barrio Callejones in Lares a soldier riding a horse went to a street stall and asked that a bottle be placed on

Rafael Ortiz

the counter. He then practiced his aim shooting at the bottle from his horse. The bullet went through the wall and wounded Sebastián Ramos in the hip. Ramos was sick and lying on a folding bed on the other side of the wall.[20] In Barros (Orocovis) a soldier mortally wounded young Arturo Vargas with a revolver. Outraged, the people demanded an investigation.[21]

In Vieques, soldier Herbert Schotte of the New York 47th, while on guard duty, killed civilian Quintín Ruiz. General Grant, recommending a court-martial to establish Schotte's innocence, said, "I recommend that Schotte be brought before a General Court-Martial so that in the future, when U. S. soldiers may not be as popular with the natives, as at the present time, he cannot be annoyed by bringing up these charges." Schotte was absolved.[22]

In Arecibo, a mounted soldier trampled and killed a child who was playing on the road. The accused soldier had had previous clashes that showed he had been "overbearing in his treatment of natives."[23] In Fajardo, Sergeant Trenchard, of the New York 47th, shot convict Fidel Gómez while Gómez was trying to escape. According to General Grant, the incident was used to "excite the more disorderly classes of people into annoying the troops at Fajardo."[24] In Adjuntas, in June 1899, a group of people trying to get economic assistance from the military authorities provoked an argument with a guard; a soldier shot and killed an elderly man named Cándido Rivera.[25] On December 5, 1899, in San Sebastián,

> soldier Charles Anderson, who was in the habit of playing with the school children during recess, somewhat drunk and believing his rifle was unloaded, aimed at the group. The children ran off in all directions, except 7-year-old Juan Evangelista Toledo, who believed this was a joke, as the soldier often gave him candy. All of a sudden a shot was heard, and Juan Evangelista fell to the ground with his chest shattered. Moments later he was dead.[26]

The internal correspondence of the commanders shows that the military government was deeply worried by the frequency of this type of incident. The high command often urged the heads of the detachments to stop abuse with firearms.

One sector of the country's public opinion was outraged at the frequent disturbances caused by the soldiers during the night and on their days off. Puerto Ricans were not used to the extroverted conduct common in the United States, even when it was not in conflict with written regulations. *La Estrella Solitaria*, reporting on a Sunday open-air concert in Ponce, wrote:

> Apparently while on duty, a captain of the American troops twice stopped a lady and a young girl who were taking a stroll arm in arm. He made disrespectful gestures unworthy of a military man who belongs to a nation that calls itself educated, powerful and great.
>
> If General Henry, who is responsible for this, does not prevent these scenes, to which the people of Ponce are not accustomed, we

will be forced to send an emphatic official complaint to the government in Washington, signed by the residents of this city.

We are not in the heart of Africa, Sirs![27]

The class-conscious language of the Ponce press did not hide the fact that the ruling class was not the only one that was offended. The soldiers, whom the officers occasionally excused, alleging that they did not know about the effects of rum, were doing damage. A particularly bitter case took place in Isabela on January 8, 1899. A dance was being held, and except for the musicians, the soldiers of Company E of the 6th Infantry Regiment stationed there were not invited. The soldiers observed the dance from the street. When it began to rain, they tried to get into the house, but somebody closed the doors. The town was disturbed with the resulting confusion and fighting. The military commander went to the scene and jailed some prominent people of Isabela that night. The furor that this action produced in the people of the town resulted in a high-level investigation. As a result of the investigation the military authorities were exonerated, and instructions were given to try the sergeant and the soldiers who had intruded into the dance.[28]

Military Discipline

All those incidents were symptomatic of the problems of military discipline that the occupation army was facing. The soldiers had unstimulating work routines. Once the need to patrol the roads and trails decreased, their main tasks were training and maintenance. Camps lacked recreational facilities and even adequate light. There were no Spanish classes or counseling services for the soldiers. Chaplains were scarce. Inevitably, at the end of the day the soldiers ended up in the town's bars and gambling houses.[29]

Due to the different languages and cultural backgrounds, the regular soldiers had difficulty mixing with the civilians. Even the religious forms observed by the Puerto Ricans seemed strange to most of them. With their own officers as well, relationships were not always easy.

During the weeks following the invasion, the Puerto Rican press commented favorably on the informal relationship between officers and enlisted men of the American volunteer forces. In some cases, as with the regiments from Illinois, the officers had been elected by the volunteers.[30]

This egalitarian treatment was not characteristic of the regular forces. Most officers did not share their housing or their food with the enlisted men. Relationships between the enlisted men and officers were often strained. Lack of discipline proliferated, and there were cases of desertion.

Courts-Martial

In view of the disciplinary problems, the military leaders tried to suppress the insubordination and delinquency of the soldiers by any means. Henry insisted on the strict application of the military code, and this resulted in numerous courts-martial. However, the frequency of the indictments and the severity of the sentences did not alleviate the disciplinary problems.

Let us take as an example the case of Private Patrick J. Hayes, of Company E of the 19th Regular Infantry Regiment. His officers found him drunk and disturbing the peace in Ponce on August 4,1898, and docked him $5 from his pay. On August 11 of the same year, he disobeyed an order and was absent without leave. He was sentenced to one month of hard labor. He was absent from camp from reveille on September 30 until 4:00 p.m. on October 1 and returned drunk. He was docked one month's pay. On October 9, he was absent at reveille and was fined $2.50 from his pay. On October 14, he was absent from assigned tasks at 7:00 a.m. and at 1:00 p.m., and was jailed for five days at hard labor. On December 1, at 12:45 p.m., he was removed drunk from the house of a civilian in Ponce. He was docked $5.00 from his pay and was in jail for five days. On December 13, he was absent from military review and was docked $10 from his pay.

Hayes was absent from camp from January 2 to 4, 1898, and for this he was fined $10 from his pay. During inspection on January 7, they found his weapon dirty and jailed him for ten days. On the night of January 29, he was absent without leave until 11 and was docked $5.00 from his pay. On January 30, he left camp even though he was under arrest and confined. He was docked one month's pay and was jailed for a month. He was absent from his company from reveille on March 10 until 4:00 p.m. of the next day. For this offense he was court-martialed on March 24. During his trial he declared:

> I am an old soldier's son, my father is dead now five years, when I wrote to my mother from St. Louis, I told her I was going to enlist, she wrote back to me and said: "If you do, come home the same as your father did." I have nothing more to say.[31]

After serving six months at hard labor in Ponce, Hayes was sentenced to a dishonorable discharge without pay. The discipline pattern in this case gives an idea of the frustration and boredom caused by the badly paid military life.

Soldier James T. Davison of Company G, 5th Cavalry, stationed in Aibonito, was court-martialed for disobedience and lack of respect toward an officer. Davison pleaded guilty, but blamed his actions on his addiction to morphine:

> About two years ago I took the cure for the opium habit. I did not touch any of it for eight or nine months. While with my regiment in Cuba the Doctor prescribed Camphor and opium pills. When I got back to the States, the habit came back on me but not so strong as when I took the cure. I have continued to use it since and meant to take the cure again as soon as I could get enough money. . . . This [sic] by the advice of Lt. Parker, G troop 5th Cav., that I make this statement now as I was ashamed to have it known.[32]

Davison was sentenced to be docked all pay less $15 and to work in prison for two months.

Courts-martial tended to be benign in cases of first offense. Still, one sometimes has the feeling that military justice was not equal for all. For example, Private Gilbert N. Riley, of the 6th Infantry Regiment, was accused of inciting his fellow soldiers to burn their tents, of telling them that their due rations were being stolen, of urging them to march through the streets as a mob, and of inducing many of them to behave seditiously. He was found guilty of inciting others, but was sentenced to only one day of confinement.[33]

Most often, court-martial sentences consisted of imprisonment with hard labor and loss of pay. Usually, prison terms were served in Ponce or San Juan, and, in the case of extended sentences, in the United States. When Henry left office, he reduced the sentences of many of the soldiers who were in jail.

The Military Re-Thinking about Puerto Rico

The naive view of Puerto Rico that some military men had during the weeks following the invasion is remarkable. However, these initial expressions rapidly gave way to greater caution, as officers assumed military command of the different municipalities and faced the complex economic and social problems of their respective zones.

Eventually, the military governor requested the military district commanders to submit reports on the country's situation. The reading of some of these reports, preserved in the National Archives in Washington, shows us different officers trying out different interpretations of the country, and attempting to propose solutions to its problems. The basic profile of Puerto Rico's economy and society may be seen in detail through the perspective of each officer. For some, merchants were the problem, and they recommended that the military government favor the hacienda owners. For others, the duty of the government was to protect the poor workers against the exploitation of the ruling class. Some believed the best action was to remove the mayors and the judges and to put military officers in charge of the details of power. Some even discovered they liked Spaniards better than Criollos. All pontificated about the possible benefits of annexing Puerto Rico to the United States. However, they were concerned about the lack of appropriate tariff agreements, the exchange of currency, the financing difficulties, and the avalanche of speculators who would come to Puerto Rico from the United States.[34]

Military City Planning

The local military commanders interfered the most in the area of city planning. Reflecting their American idea of city life, several officers interfered in the life of the towns. Some commanders imposed the law, passed later, that ordered that stores be closed on Sundays.[35] Merchants complained about the adoption of a closing practice that harmed their interests. Many farmers were used to shopping on Sundays when they came to town to hear mass. Closing the stores in town on Sunday encouraged the development of rural stores that could compete better with the urban stores, and that were less subject to the supervision of the authorities.

The friction caused by the military-imposed Sunday closing was only one of the conflicts produced by the combination of a military calendar, schedule, and sense of time, which differed from that of the Criollos. The siesta clashed with the military schedule. The time for socializing during the evening was defined in two different ways. In the first year of occupation, the Americans insisted on celebrating Thanksgiving, Washington's birthday and the Fourth of July; the Criollos in Ponce refused to open the stores on Three Kings Day, 1899.

On April 1, 1899, the inter-colonial time of the 60th meridian took effect; the time was communicated daily to all telegraph offices. In Mayagüez, Colonel Carr worried because not all the clocks in the city showed the same time. He instructed the mayor to order that the church clock show "inter-colonial time" and insisted that the San Juan telegraph office provide the correct time. However, the Signal Corps, guardians of the official time, told him that the Mayagüez clocks did not work properly and that "Inferior clocks were furnished, but good ones will be obtained and distributed as soon as practicable. Time is sent over all wires at exact noon and correct time can be had at any telegraph office at that hour."[36]

The idea of space among the American military also challenged the assumptions underlying the way in which the ruling classes used urban spaces. Shortly after the invasion, the Ponce and Mayagüez newspapers began complaining about street-walkers who no longer respected the old boundaries to which they had been confined; about children, who played and ran on areas of the plaza previously banned to them; about disrespectful individuals, who following the example of the American troops were now less deferential; and above all, about the *tortoleños*, Caribbean immigrants who had arrived after the invasion and had filled the streets and the poor areas with their strange accents. Different ideas on the use of space in the urban areas caused conflicts. The military intervention in the daily life of Ponce, Mayagüez and other cities placed the ideas of the ruling class in question. It would be interesting to follow these conflicts step by step.

Another concern of the military was public hygiene.[37] The military government implemented a massive smallpox vaccination program. There were municipal provisions to regulate the location of outhouses, the collection of garbage, and the raising of animals in the towns. However, the extent of the rules and their fulfillment varied widely from one municipality to another. Some military commanders undertook an aggressive campaign regarding these matters, trying to guarantee a modicum of public health. This aggressiveness produced some reactions. For example, in Barros (Orocovis) the mayor ordered that a latrine belonging to the military be dismantled, alleging they were not caring for it adequately. This wounded the military's pride and provoked letters to the military governor requesting that the mayor be fired.[38] It was surprising how ready and willing the military was to engage in this type of farce.

Some military commanders, mostly those of Isabela and Yauco, were shocked that mentally ill people were not locked up:

> I respectfully call attention to the fact that there are a large number of persons in this and the other towns of my command who are of unsound mind they have been allowed at large the local authorities have no places to properly care for them . . . our men being unfamiliar with the language are apt to resent acts on their part for which these poor people are not responsible. The authorities should be directed to make proper provision for these cases.[39]

Cruelty to animals was another object of military concern. One of Miles' last orders before leaving Puerto Rico was to stop the use of sharp goads when driving ox carts. The commanders of the cavalry detachments were extremely sensitive to the mistreatment inflicted by riders on their mounts. During the coffee harvest of 1898–99, Captain Vernou, who was in charge of the Yauco military post, ordered the inspection of the mule trains that arrived in the city to see if they were loaded properly. This caused some conflict with the owners of the mule trains and with the hacienda owners who rented them.[40]

Not all military commanders shared the same enthusiasm for urban improvements in their districts. The commander in Lares, for example, even wrote in 1899 that there was no need for public works in that city. According to him, the streets were wide enough; the hospital had adequate capacity; the church did not need repairs; the English teachers did not need to have houses built for them, and in any case, the government should not pay for them. In Yauco, however, Captain Vernou displayed an ambitious plan to beautify the city and began to put it into practice with a committee of wealthy people. Some of the improvements he claimed to have initiated included the planting of trees and gardens, the widening of streets, the removal of rubble, the installation of public lighting, and the repairing of the plaza.[41]

The Military and the Press

During the decades 1880 and 1890, a combative press developed in Puerto Rico. Besides fighting censure, the newspapers continually faced lawsuits against their columnists from government and church officials. Immediately after the invasion some of the already existing newspapers acquired new vigor, and new ones were founded. In January 1899, Governor Henry ordered the Secretary of Justice "to dismiss the criminal prosecutions initiated for crimes of the press during the prior regime."[42] However, to the surprise of many journalists whose Jacobinic views led them to see freedom as the product of the success of the invasion, the American military did not prove to be patient with the press.

On August 19, Adjutant General Gilmore ordered Captain French, of the 19th Infantry, to close down the Ponce newspaper *La Estrella*

Solitaria, and to arrest its editor Luis Cabalier and the author of the article entitled "Venganza" ["Vengeance"]. The article asked for reprisals against the Spaniards for the deaths in Ciales on August 13. By August 22, Gilmore had lifted the restrictions on the newspaper.[43]

The Ponce newspaper *La Bomba*, whose editor was Evaristo Izcoa Díaz, published an article on October 18, censuring the vandalism of the American soldiers in Playa de Ponce. Because of this, General Henry, then commander of the Ponce military district, suppressed the newspaper.[44] On November 21, 1898, the general ordered the suppression of the newspaper *Bandera Americana*. On December 9, the Mayagüez newspaper *La Información* was suppressed, also on Henry's orders. That month he stated in the *New York Herald*: "Publication of articles criticizing those in authority and reflecting upon the government or its officers will not be allowed." On February 24, 1899, by Henry's express orders, the Ponce newspaper *La Metralla* was closed. The newspaper had included a Spanish version of the statement: "Accusations supported by evidence will always be well received if they are presented in the appropriate manner, but their publication will result in the suppression of the guilty newspaper."[45]

On March 6, Captain Vernou, the commander in Yauco, asked the commander in Ponce to warn Francisco Gaudier that he had five days to withdraw a statement in an article entitled "Injusticia" ["Injustice"], published in *La Democracia* on February 28. In the article, Gaudier claimed that the American troops had caused property damage. The author refused to recant, and Vernou filed libel charges against him.[46] On March 10, the commander in Mayagüez gave the owner of *El Imparcial* in Mayagüez a warning from Henry for having reprinted an article from *La Correspondencia de Puerto Rico* entitled "La Guerra en las Filipinas" ["The War in the Philippines"]. In the warning, Henry said that

> Its spirit is so manifestly hostile that the appearance of similar articles will lead to action against the paper. You will warn the editor of this and impress on him the importance of refraining from even indirect attacks on the troops of the Republic here or elsewhere.[47]

About the warning to *El Imparcial*, another Mayagüez newspaper, *El Territorio*, wrote, "Given the narrow sphere in which the press works today, it is impossible to comment."

After Henry was relieved of office, reprisals against the newspapers decreased somewhat. During this truce, Evaristo Izcoa Díaz began publishing another newspaper, this time under the name of *El Combate*. Barely three weeks had passed following the first issue when General Davis sent Izcoa a letter:

> You should be careful not to abuse your privileges by publishing seditious statements tending to spread false ideas and incite an uprising or a civil war. These discussions should be characterized by calm, temperance, sincerity and honesty. . . . As long as the press keeps its arguments within the reasonable limits of moderation and honesty indicated here, it will find protection and support. I trust that you will realize perfectly the limitation of the press regarding this matter....[48]

Not only was the newspaper suppressed that year, but Izcoa was charged and jailed. The reason was an article, considered libelous, written against the proposal of corporal punishment.[49] In December, the director of *La Vanguardia* was called to the Ponce Court "to state the name of the author of the article entitled 'El crimen de un guardia' [A Guard's Crime'], published in that newspaper."[50]

The military governors also resented the articles published in the American press about their administration. On October 31, 1898, General Henry, then commander of the Ponce military district, recommended to General Brooke that he file charges against the *Baltimore American* for an article about the conditions of the military hospital in Ponce. On January 1, 1899, Henry, then governor, and Grant, commander of the San Juan military district, instructed the commander in Ponce to arrest Arthur B. Jack, a reporter for the *New York Journal*. They alleged that "He has started several false reports which are doing harm." Two days later instructions were given to the commanders in Carolina and Fajardo to arrest Jack on charges of having taken a bicycle in San Juan without its owner's permission. He was arrested in Caguas.[51]

The Military and Hurricane San Ciriaco

By June 1899, the people in Puerto Rico were disheartened because Congress was taking too long to pass the laws needed to regulate commerce between Puerto Rico and the United States. The new tariff agreements with Spain and Cuba were very harmful to Puerto Rican coffee, which now had to compete to get into some markets that were certain before. The public works programs of Governors Henry and Davis had not satisfied the country's great need for employment. The climate for investment was extremely negative. In these circumstances it seemed that the country was likely to be shaken again by social upheaval.

To make things worse, on August 8, Hurricane San Ciriaco devastated crops and livestock, destroyed a good part of the houses and roads, and plunged Puerto Rico into one of the most disastrous situations in its history.

Reports from the districts most affected began to arrive at La Fortaleza, the Governor's office. Ponce had suffered a terrible flood. Great confusion prevailed in the city, and it took a long time to establish the number of dead and missing. The drinking water system was interrupted. Dead animals rotted in the streets and in the countryside. Thousands of people crowded into the public buildings asking for food and shelter. Contagious diseases began to spread. Arecibo had suffered an enormous flood of the Río Grande. In Aibonito the coffee had been totally destroyed, and there was no food available. In Utuado the ravages were so great that an estimate of the losses could only be done slowly. Heavy rains made rivers rise in an unexpected and unprecedented way.[52]

In such desperate circumstances, the country, deprived of political power, impoverished, demoralized, and miserable, faced the task of reconstruction. The material help offered by the military government to the dispossessed was conditional upon their working on the farms. In other words, the food distributed, although in no way a substitute for wages, was given on condition that the head of the household be working. Exceptions were made only in cases of extreme poverty, when there was no one in the family able to work.[53]

In the coffee-growing area—the most affected by the hurricane—these remedies could only alleviate things, since landowners did not have the capital or the credit to undertake the reconstruction of their farms. Therefore, the prospects were that it would take several years before their coffee farms would be in full production again. Hacienda owners could offer little to their *agregados* besides the assurance of a place to rebuild their huts. In short, the military government provided the food, and in that way the state displaced the landowners as providers of essential goods to workers. This situation should be studied carefully in a history of the development of the state in Puerto Rico.

There were some bands after San Ciriaco in the coffee-growing area.[54] However, the effects of the hurricane, added to the repressive force of the state, ended up breaking the resistance that the "landless" had exercised against the economic system in the coffee-growing areas. In the midst of their poverty and their outdated resources, the workers and the small landowners turned to the military government for food and jobs in public works. The military government then, through its actions, reinstated the landowners as arbiters of the rural system, as providers of employment and security, and as guarantors of the personal conduct of their *agregados*. In such circumstances, both landowners and workers surrendered to the new political rule, which had been made overwhelming by the hurricane.

The Military and the Americanization of Puerto Rico

Usually the beginning of the process of Americanization in Puerto Rico is dated from the time of the military government. Undoubtedly, this period gave a strong impetus to the Americanization of the country, but interestingly enough some consumers' habits and some attitudes later identified with the Americanization process preceded the American invasion.

For example, newspaper advertisements during the decade 1890 promoted all kinds of American goods. Not even the war could stop the advertisement of Scott's Emulsion and other American products in the newspapers.[55] Baseball was an established sport in Puerto Rico even before July 25, 1898.[56] Bicycle tours were reported in the newspapers. The

Puerto Ricans who were studying for degrees in the United States had already introduced American idiomatic expressions, as may be verified in the articles they wrote for the newspapers. The dollar was the usual currency of reference, and pleasure trips to the United States were frequent. The people had already begun copying the lifestyles that prevailed in the United States.

This process was greatly accelerated immediately after the invasion. Newspaper advertisements for lessons and courses, and grammars and dictionaries, showed the enormous enthusiasm the Puerto Ricans had for learning English. Very soon conspicuous imitation of American tastes began. In October 1898, a person asked the United States authorities to let him change his name from Eduardo to Edward.[57] As usual, exaggerated imitations multiplied, and soon the less skillful imitators were the target of sarcasm.

It is interesting to point out the things that were considered typically American and worthy of imitation. Egalitarism became fashionable. The newspaper *La Bomba*, for example, criticized the Ponce municipal government for still wanting to be referred to as "Your Excellency" when they were now living in the republican era. *La Bruja*, in Mayagüez, even suggested completely new names for places in the city, to reflect the advent of freedom.[58] American sports became popular. *El Combate*, always class-conscious and stubbornly anticlerical, noted that the soldiers had made bicycles popular in Ponce, and that these could be rented for 30 cents an hour. It said that "even cooks and beggars now go to market and to beg, respectively, riding swift bicycles. . . . As for priests, they can ride women's bicycles."[59] Bitter controversies broke out regarding whether bicycle riding caused permanent damage to the knees. The elite was initiated into poker. In Ponce, in February 1899, the police detained "Celedonia Mateo for being dressed as a man, terrifying passers-by at eleven o'clock at night."[60]

There was an interesting debate about the religion of the Americans. Catholic priests hurried to point out that there were practicing Catholics among the Americans. The sight of the Irish soldiers taking communion at High Mass, in towns where few men took communion, was the subject of moralizing commentary.[61] But, on the other hand, most military men were Protestants, among them, the ones of the highest rank. Americanization and Protestanization were seen as simultaneous processes.[62]

The problem of the reorganization of the public education system in relation to the Americanization program of the military government led to debates in the press. The military actively directed the program to distribute American flags to the schools, supported by groups of veterans in the United States.[63] They developed a whole civic ritual around the handing over of the flags. In Yauco, the ceremony was held on Christmas day, at nine o'clock in the morning, with all the teachers and the students of the district present.[64] This would be a fertile subject for a study on the history of attitudes.

The implementation of the Americanization program did not have the unanimous support of the military. One or another expressed qualms about being assigned tasks for which he had not been trained, and which were not part of his job.[65] Yet, at least in their internal communications, most officers used the annexionist discourse that was being made popular in the United States by a new generation of Republican politicians, such as Beveridge and Theodore Roosevelt.[66]

The political tasks the military had to assume in Puerto Rico were nothing new in a country that had lived for so long under Spanish military governors. For the American military, however, it represented a return to the time of the Reconstruction of the South after the Civil War. That model entailed great inconvenience for Puerto Rican civilians, who did not consider themselves to have been defeated in the war. Those who had believed the invasion would bring a rapid establishment of American political institutions were disconcerted at the slowness of the transition to civil government.

After June 1900, most troops left the island. Still, military enclaves remained in places where the Americanizing mentality of the period of military government lasted. Isolated from the rest of the country, oblivious to the great ideas of the political debates, alienated by the fast economic changes around them, the anachronistic military camps remained. They continued to worship an ideology that not even Reagan, with his baroque prose about the Republican restoration, was able to revive. The sentries of the remaining bases and camps denied entrance to modern Puerto Rico. Like the last Roman legionnaires on Hadrian's Wall, they continued to wait for the end of the war after the war.

In April 2004, the last American base, Roosevelt Roads, closed.

CHAPTER SEVEN

Conclusion

After the 1898 invasion, the "seditious bands" were the broadest and most vigorous expression of popular sentiment as a reaction to the Spanish-American war in Puerto Rico. However, far from being a resistance movement against the invasion, the bands represented the repudiation of the previous economic and social regime, and a settlement of accounts with the most visible representatives of that regime.

The main field of operations of the bands was the coffee-growing area in the interior of the island. The most violent manifestations of social conflict arose where the loss of inherited land and the subordination to hacienda work and to indebtedness were recent events. The favorite targets of the attacks of the *tiznados* were rural stores, warehouses, machinery houses, and the homes of the hacienda owners. Former rural guards, hacienda overseers, and clerks of the hacienda stores occasionally suffered the violence of the bands. Hacienda owners and merchants were present at some of the attacks, and several were murdered, beaten and humiliated. However, the violence of the bands was concentrated primarily on the symbols of domination. They burned account books, machinery to remove the pulp from coffee, warehouses, and furnishings in the hacienda houses. Frequently, they stole stored coffee, food, and clothes from the hacienda owners.

Once the bands were disassociated from their original role as auxiliaries of the invading forces, they were composed mostly of small landowners and their sons, day laborers and *agregados*, and some soldiers discharged from the Criollo troops that had been auxiliaries of the Spanish troops. It is interesting to note the leadership the small landowners displayed in this situation, leading workers from other areas of production.

During the first phase of the bands, in other words, from August to the first weeks of October, the object of the attacks was property belonging to the Spaniards. However, as the movement gained strength, and as the vulnerability of the landowners in the mountains became more evident, the farms and stores belonging to the Criollos also became targets of the bands' attacks. The character of the bands' actions as social struggle became more evident when the contrast between Spaniards and Criollos lessened. In such circumstances, both Spanish and Criollo landowners sought the protection of the army of invasion.

American troops intervened to guarantee the safety of the rich and powerful and to protect their property. This intervention restored the presence and power of the state in the coffee-growing area. Its most lasting consequence was the support of the rich and powerful for the new regime. The hacienda owners and the merchants perceived the presence of the American troops on the island as a necessary balance to the evident strength of the small landowners and the workers in the mountain ranges. The acts of the bands had dispelled the illusion that the *jíbaro*, or the person living in the mountains, was passive, fatalistic, resigned, and had no ideas of his own. As a result, the *jíbaro* came to be feared, and the latent threat of the rural masses was used as justification for the continuation of the military regime.

For the Americans, the bands revealed another aspect of the people whom, they claimed, they were trying to free from ignorance and illness. The regular troops that replaced the voluntary soldiers of the invasion had a model at hand to explain the seditious behavior of the *jíbaros*. After all, these troops had spent long years in the American West battling the Indians. Soon they established the similarity between the seditious *jíbaros* and the Indians.

As with the Indians, was not the best way to assure their docility to guarantee them food, health and welfare? Hence, General Henry tried to provide employment for them in public works. He also displayed a marked effort to eradicate smallpox and to satisfy the basic requirements of public hygiene. These measures effectively reduced the bands and made them disappear. In June 1899, General Davis wanted to end this experiment in public welfare managed by the military. On August 8, however, the hurricane occurred. The impact of Hurricane San Ciriaco forced the military to focus again on the desperate condition of the masses. The assistance programs after the hurricane definitely identified the new regime with a paternalism never known before in Puerto Rico.

For the Americans, the bands divided the invaded country into two types of areas. One was the urban coastal area, reminiscent of the Spain of Washington Irving and Prescott. The other was the mountains, poor, rebellious, similar to the ranges of the wild Indians in the American West. In the eyes of investors, the mountains were dangerous, treacherous, cunning and backward. It was better to leave them to their fate, and to concentrate the energy and resources of the great colonizing project on the coast.

The decapitalization of coffee helped place the industry in the hands of the Criollos. The product that had been identified with Corsicans and Majorcans very soon became the Criollo product par excellence, but of secondary importance for national production. The descendants of Corsicans and Majorcans, accepted as natives now that coffee was a Criollo industry, found their Puerto Rican roots when their main economic activity lost its importance.

Hurricane San Ciriaco accelerated the process of making the coast the productive sector and the mountains the economically backward area. For the rural population it was a signal for a massive return to the coast. The ruined landowners and the remaining *agregados* in the end played down their differences. Although the conflicts never disappeared, the rhetoric of social harmony covered the naked evidence of the battles recently fought. This way, the myth of a harmonious and patriarchal coffee plantation was gradually created. The collective memory of the bands would be toned down, and only the memory of some cases, of some Spaniards, of some weeks after the invasion, would be remembered.

Why Remember Them?

To remember the bands is, first of all, to reveal the conflictive character of the old economic rule in the mountains. Likewise, it is to acknowledge the fighting capacity of the people of the mountains against those who had dispossessed them by subjecting them to the work regime of the haciendas and the indebtedness to hacienda stores. Revenge for the *compontes*, a torture device used in 1887, and for the economic exploitation of the previous decades emphasized the depth of the social divisions in the country. It also showed how inadequate and superficial the autonomic regime of 1898 was in terms of leading the country to social peace. To study the bands is a necessary stage in the process of demythologizing a history we have inherited, a history that insists on finding the key to our past only in the political decisions supported or approved by the metropolis.

The bands also constitute an eloquent testimony to the conflict of mentalities brought about by the invasion. The old clashes between Criollos and Spaniards caused by different ideas about land, work, honor, and courage arose again, with new force. Initially, the conflicts occurred in conditions that were more advantageous to the Criollos. Soon, however, it was evident that the conflicts were not about ethnic values and codes anymore, but about social attitudes. These attitudes were counteracted, in turn, by those of the invaders, who were the guarantors of law and order. In this theater, three types of opposition succeeded one another with surprising speed. In each act of the social drama, the workers and the *jíbaro* small landowners represented the role of challengers of the prevailing political values. Social peace, imposed in spite of their hostile activity, was achieved without them. However, it allotted to them—as a reluctant acknowledgment of their capacity to jeopardize the institutional order—economic opportunities, social assistance, and the possibility of political participation. This implied the eventual breakdown of the economic system which had been restored.

Abbreviations

Adjuntas Letters Sent	NARA, RG 395, entry 5868, Adjuntas Letters Sent from May 24, 1899 to July 25, 1900.
AGPR	Puerto Rico General Archives (Archivo General de Puerto Rico).
Aguadilla Letters Received	NARA, RG 395, entry 5875, Letters Received Aguadilla, PR 1898 1899 1900 and Telegrams Received Aguadilla P. R. 1898–1900.
Aguadilla Letters Sent	NARA, RG 395, entry 5871. Post of Aguadilla (Company H 11th Infantry) Letters Sent. Vol. 1: Nov. 1898–July 1899. Vol. 2: July 1899–July 1900.
Aibonito Letters Sent	NARA, RG 395, entry 5881, Aibonito, Puerto Rico Letters Sent. 2 vols.: 1899–1900.
AMP	Ponce Municipal Archives (Archivo Municipal de Ponce).
Arecibo Letters Sent	NARA, RG 395, entry 5890, Post of Arecibo, Company Letters Sent. March 1899–March 1900.
CFRU	AGPR, Fondo de Obras Públicas, Catastro de Fincas Rústicas de Utuado.
FGEPR	Fondo de Gobernadores Españoles de Puerto Rico, Archivo Histórico.

General Orders   NARA, RG 395, entry 5841, General Orders and
                        Circulars, Headquarters Department of Puerto Rico,
                        Office of the Military Governor 1898 and 1899 (1 vol.)

Headquarters   NARA, RG 108, entry 122, Headquarters of the Army in
Letters Received   the Field. Letters and Telegrams Received. Vols. 188–191.

Headquarters   NARA, RG 108, entry 119, Headquarters of the Army in
Letters Sent   the Field, Vols. 184–187.

Lares Letters Sent   NARA, RG 395, entry 5900. Post Letters Sent Lares
                        Puerto Rico: 8 Feb. 1899 To: 7 Mar. 1900.

Mayagüez Letters   NARA, RG 2 385 entry 5908, Mayagüez, P. R. + West.
Received   Dist. of P. R. Letters Received. Boxes 1–3.

Mayagüez Letters   NARA, RG 395, entry 5904, Post of Mayagüez.
Sent   Letters Sent. 5 vols.

NARA   National Archives and Records Administration,
                        Washington, D.C.

Padrón 1900   AGPR, Fondo de Obras Públicas, Propiedad Pública,
                        Utuado, exp. 170, "Relación de los terratenientes que . . ."

Ponce Letters   NARA, RG 395, entry 5866. Letters received, Troops in
Received   the Field From: Sept. 1898–To: March 1899 [Ponce.]

Ponce Letters Sent   NARA, RG 395, entry 5928. Post of Ponce, Letters Sent.
                        4 vols.

Puerto Rico   NARA, RG 395, entry 5837. Headquarters Department of
Letters Received   Porto Rico, Adjutant General's Office, Letters Received.
                        1898: vols. 2–9 [vol. 1 is missing.]

RG   Record Group [at NARA]

San Juan Letters Sent	NARA, RG 395, entry 5867, Letters Sent, District of San Juan. Vol. 1: From October 1898 to Jan. 1899. Vol. 2: From: 17 January 1898 to: 12 April 1899.
Special Orders	Department of Porto Rico, Special Orders 1898–1899.
TSA	Fondo del Tribunal Superior de Arecibo, AGPR.
Vieques Letters Received	NARA, RG 395, entry 5956, Vieques Letters Received, District of San Juan. From: Jan. 1899 to May 1899.
Yauco Letters Received	NARA, RG 395, entry 5958, Letters Received, Post of Yauco, vols. 1–3.
Yauco Letters Sent	NARA, RG 395, entry 5957, Letters Sent, Post of Yauco From: Oct. 1898 To: June 1899.

Notes

NOTES TO THE PREFACE

1. NARA, RG 395, entry 5858, "Miscellaneous Letters," copy of the record of the August 14, 1898, proceedings of the town council of Cabo Rojo.

NOTES TO CHAPTER ONE

1. Pedro Albizu-Campos, *Obras Escogidas*, ed. Benjamín Torres (San Juan, 1981), vol. 2, p. 15; vol. 3, pp. 22–23, 64, 99.

2. See bibliography for the work of these authors.

3. See Cayetano Coll y Toste, *Reseña de estado social, económico e industrial de la Isla de Puerto Rico al tomar posesión de ella los Estados Unidos* (San Juan, 1899); United States War Department, *Report on the Census of Porto Rico, 1899* (Washington, 1900).

4. See Andrés Ramos-Mattei, *La hacienda azucarera: Su crecimiento y crisis en Puerto Rico (siglo xix)* (San Juan, 1981); Carlos Casanova, "Propiedad agrícola y poder en el municipio de Manatí: 1885–1898" (M.A. thesis in History, University of Puerto Rico [UPR], 1985); Cruz Ortiz-Cuadra, "Crédito y azúcar: Los hacendados de Humacao ante la crisis del dulce: 1865–1900" (M.A. thesis in History, UPR, 1985).

5. See Guillermo Baralt, *Yauco o las minas de oro cafetaleras (1756–1898)*, 2d ed., rev. (San Juan, 1984); Laird W. Bergad, *Coffee and the Growth of Agrarian Capitalism in Nineteenth Century Puerto Rico* (Princeton, 1983); Carlos Buitrago, *Haciendas Cafetaleras y clases terratenientes en el Puerto Rico decimonónico* (Río Piedras, 1982); Vivian Carro, "La formación de la gran propiedad cafetalera: la hacienda Pietri," *Anales de Investigación Histórica* 2, no. 1 (Jan.–June, 1975); Luis E. Díaz, *Castañer: Una hacienda cafetalera en Puerto Rico (1868–1930)*, 2d ed. (Río Piedras, 1983).

6. See Peter Katsilis Morales, "Economía y sociedad del pueblo de Camuy, 1850–1868" (M. A. Thesis in History, UPR, 1986). Corozal at the end of the 19th and beginning of the 20th centuries is the subject of a thesis by Rafael Cabrera.

7. See José Ramón Abad, *Puerto Rico en la feria exposición de Ponce en 1882,* 2nd ed. (Río Piedras, 1967), p. 225, and Fernando López-Tuero, *La reforma agrícola* (San Juan, 1891).

8. *Cuerdas* [.97 acre] of land under cultivation in Utuado, 1851 and 1897:

	Coffee	Cereal grains and minor crops
1851	1,491	6,543
1897	15,883	4,874

("Riqueza Agrícola del Pueblo de Utuado, 1851," in *FMU;* Jorge Saldaña, *Café en Puerto Rico* [San Juan, 1935], p. 15).

9. Henry K. Carroll, *Report on the Island of Porto Rico* (Washington, 1899), p. 48.

10. See Ramos-Mattei, p. 25. In *Worker in the Cane* (New Haven, 1960), Sidney Mintz explains in detail how precarious life was in the countryside during the off-season in the 1940s.

11. See Díaz, pp. 53–55; Bergad, pp. 197–98; Carlos Buitrago, *Los orígenes históricos de la sociedad precapitalista en Puerto Rico* (Río Piedras, 1976), pp. 27–28, 40–42.

12. Ibid., 44.

13. See Ana Mercedes Santiago de Curet, "Crédito, moneda y bancos en Puerto Rico durante el siglo xix" (M. A. Thesis in History, UPR, 1978).

14. See Coll y Toste, pp. 19–20.

15. See Loida Figueroa, *Breve Historia de Puerto Rico,* part 2, *Desde el crepúsculo del dominio español hasta la antesala de la Ley Foraker, 1892–1900* (Río Piedras, 1977), pp. 26 ff.

16. Coll y Toste, pp. 21–22.

17. By way of example, Bergad uses the case of Juan Sella, who in 1882 paid Castañer Hermanos six Puerto Rican pesos to haul approximately 49 and a half hundredweights of coffee from his farm to the Castañer warehouse, 75 cents per hundredweight to haul the same load from Barrio Bartolo to Yauco, and 20 cents per hundredweight from Yauco to Ponce (Bergad, p. 158).

18. Guadalupe Rivera wrote a monograph entitled "La carretera #9," while at UPR-Río Piedras. [In the author's personal files.—Tr.].

19. See Edwin Borrero, "El ferrocarril de circunvalación: Estudio de una subcultura puertorriqueña y la tecnología auxiliar (1888–1898)" (M. A. Thesis in History, UPR, 1977).

20. See María de los Angeles Castro, "La construcción de la carretera central en Puerto Rico (siglo xix)" (M. A. Thesis in History, UPR, 1969).

21. "Embarking for Puerto Rico," *New York Times*, July 19, 1898, p. 1.

22. *La Correspondencia*, October 23, 1895, p. 2.

23. "Ecce Homo," *La Democracia*, October 29, 1898, p. 2.

24. See the 1895 issues of *La Bomba* in the Puerto Rican Collection of Sacred Heart University, San Juan.

25. See Gervasio García and A. G. Quintero-Rivera, *Desafío y solidaridad* (Río Piedras, 1982), chapters 1 and 2.

26. *La Correspondencia*, April 28, 1892, p. 2.

27. Germán Delgado-Passapera, *Puerto Rico: Sus luchas emancipadoras (1850–1898)* (Río Piedras, 1984), pp. 427–29, 473–76.

28. *El Buscapié*, September 24, 1895, p. 2.

29. See Díaz, pp. 56–57; Buitrago, *Los orígenes*, pp. 39–40; FGEPR, box 379, official report to the governor, dated February 1, 1895, on the fire that razed 40 *cuerdas* of sugar cane at Hacienda "La Estrella" in Playa de Ponce.

30. *El Buscapié*, November 29, 1895, p. 2.

31. See, for example, the declarations regarding farmworkers implicated in the "*Sucesos*"—events—of Arroyo in 1895, in Lidio Cruz Monclova, *Historia de Puerto Rico (siglo xix)*, vol. 3, part 2 (Río Piedras, 1962), pp. 302–304.

32. See, for example, what was said about the Arroyo farmworkers in *El Buscapié* ("Croniquita Lo de Arroyo," October 25, 1895, p. 2): "That society— for lack of a better word—was made up of miserable day laborers from the countryside, incapable of any purpose but foolishness, since there can only be real conspiracy where there are ideas"; in *La Correspondencia* (October 24, 1895, p. 2): "most of the arrested men are relatively unimportant persons who do not even know how to read or write. . ."; and in *La Democracia* (October 28, 1895, p. 2): "poor frightened *jíbaros*. . ." In 1898 Evaristo Izcoa wrote in *La Bomba,* (Sept, 29, 1989, p. 1): "Our poor *jíbaro*, that living automaton, that backward human being who has only natural instincts—which are not always the best—to guide his development, barely realizes what goes on around him."

NOTES TO CHAPTER TWO

1. "Por el campo," *El País*, May 18, 1898, p. 1.

2. Ibid., May 26 and 30, 1898, p. 2.

3. *La Unión*, July 9, 1898, p. 3.

4. Carl Sandburg, *Always the Young Strangers* (New York, 1953), p. 416.

5. National Archives, Washington, D. C., RG 395, entry 5857: "General Schwann's Report of Operations in the Campaign in Puerto Rico," p. 4.

6. *La Correspondencia*, August 20, 1898, p. 3.

7. *El País*, October 10, 1898, p. 3.

8. "Ecos de Vega Baja," *La Bruja*, April 17, 1898, p. 4.

9. "Zurra Literaria," *La Bruja*, May 8, 1898, p. 2.

10. "Laboratorio de bolas," *La Bruja*, May 8, 1898, pp. 1–2.

11. "Bien," *El País*, April 25, 1898, p. 2.

12. "Manatí," ibid, p. 2.

13. "Utuado," *La Correspondencia*, June 13, 1898, p. 2.

14. Headquarters Letters Received, vol. 188, p. 22.

15. See Henry F. Keenan, *The Conflict With Spain: A History of the War Based Upon Official Reports and Descriptions of Eye-Witnesses* (Philadelphia, 1898), pp. 471–73; Headquarters Letters Received, vol. 188, p. 47.

16. The Governor General of Puerto Rico, Macías, was of the same opinion. See Carmelo Rosario Natal, *Puerto Rico y la crisis de la Guerra Hispanoamericana* (Hato Rey, 1975), p. 220.

17. See Newton F. Tolman, *The Search for General Miles* (New York, 1968), pp. 20–21.

18. See Headquarters Letters Sent, vol. 185, pp. 81, 82, 85, 88, 103, 104, 107.

19. Tolman, pp. 30–31.

20. See Robert L. Beisner, *Twelve Against Empire: The Anti-Imperialists, 1898–1900* (New York, 1968).

21. See correspondence in Headquarters Letters Received, vol. 188 and Headquarters Letters Sent, vol. 184.

22. See G. J. A. O'Toole, *The Spanish War: An American Epic, 1898* (New York, 1984), pp. 199, 229 ff.

23. Headquarters Letters Received, vol. 188, p. 61; Headquarters Letters Sent, vol. 184, p. 27; RG, entry 5857, "Miscellaneous Reports," copy of a letter from Secretary of Defense Alger to Miles; "Brooke to Puerto Rico," *New York Times*, July 1, 1898.

24. "San Juan's Turn Now: Puerto Rican Expedition to go Forward at Once," *New York Times*, July 15, 1898, p. 3.

25. See *New York Times*, "Woes of the Fifth Illinois, not Co. Culver's Influence, Said to Have Kept the Regiment at Home," July 29, 1898, p. 1.

26. Telegram from Alger to Miles, Headquarters Letters Received, vol. 189, p. 57; Robert Seager II and Doris Maguire, eds., *Letters and Papers of Alfred Thayer Mahan* (Annapolis, 1975), vol. 2, 573; "General Miles Places Blame," *New York Times*, August 24, 1898, p. 1; Angel Rivero, *Crónica de la Guerra Hispanoamericana en Puerto Rico* (San Juan, 1972), pp. 206–207.

27. Tolman, pp. 215–15.

28. Rivero, pp. 182–83; "Miles' Move a Surprise," *New York Times*, July 27, 1898, p. 1: "The neighborhood of Guanica and Ponce is said to be the section of

the island where the opposition to Spanish rule is strongest and where a propaganda in favor of accepting the Americans as deliverers instead of as enemies could be most advantageously begun. Gen. Miles has with him some representatives of the Puerto Rican Revolutionary Junta. It is believed that one of his objects in touching near Ponce is to establish contact with the insurgents and set on foot a movement which may result in making the American occupation of the island much easier than it would be if all the efforts of the invaders were confined to fighting their way along. Gen. Miles had a number of conferences with representatives of the revolutionists of the island before he left here, and he is known to have counted on doing as much toward winning over the people of the province by friendly overture as possible, having regard to the ultimate benefit of such a policy on the permanent American rule, which it is proposed to establish here." Miles declared to the Associated Press correspondent: "Guanica and Cinga [sic] are in the disinfected portion of the island. Matteo [sic], the insurgent leader lives at Yauco, a few Miles inland. Had we landed at Cape San Juan a line of rifle pits might have stopped our advance." ("Our Flag Raised in Puerto Rico," ibid., p. 1). In his second autobiography (the first one was from before 1898) Miles repeated the arguments he had invoked for the press in 1898 (Nelson A. Miles, *Serving the Republic*, [New York:1911] pp. 296–97).

29. See William Wallace Whitelock, "How Guanica Was Taken," *New York Times*, August 10, 1898, p. 5.

30. Frank E. Edwards, *The '98 Campaign of the 6th Massachussetts, U. S. V.* (Boston, 1899), pp. 86–87; see Sandburg, op. cit. p. 414.

31. Headquarters Letters Received, vol. 189, pp. 57, 71; "Henry Found No Spaniards," *New York Times,* August 1, 1898, p. 1; "The Comic Side of The War," ibid., Part 2, p. 16; Edwards, p. 94.

32. See "Copy of the Report Sent to Her Majesty's Consulate by Mr. Vice-Consul Fernando M. Toro, on the invasion of the district of Ponce, Porto Rico, by the Forces of the United States of America," in Albert E. Lee, *An Island Grows* (San Juan, 1963), "Appendix I," pp. 135–42; "Sobre 'llegada de los Americanos' a esta Ciudad," AMP, Asuntos Varios, sheaf 159, dossier 178; see also "Virtud de acuerdo del Ayuntamiento disponiendo se entregue a los miembros del cuerpo Consular, Don Fernando C. Toro, Don Pedro Rosaly, Don Enrique C. Fritzi y al ciudadano inglés Don Roberto Graham una medalla de oro a cada uno por el decidido y valioso concurso que prestaron para conseguir se rindiera a los americanos de una manera honrosa esta Plaza el día 28 de Julio," ibid.., dossier 162; see also Rivero, pp. 224 ff.; see also Socorro Girón, *El Teatro La Perla y 'La Campaña de la Almudana'* (Ponce, 1986), pp. 343 A ff.; see also "The Surrender of Ponce," *New York Times*, July 30, 1898, p. 6.

33. Headquarters Letters Received, vol. 189, p. 65.

34. William Wallace Whitelock, "The Capture of Arroyo," *New York Times,* July 30, 1898, p. 4; Headquarters Letters Sent, vol. 185, p. 109; RG 395, entry 5852, "Special Field Return of US Troops at Arroyo, P. R., for August 3, 1898," "Trimonthly Field Return of U.S. Troops at Guayama, PR Commanded by Major General John R. Brooke, USA, for August 31st 1898" and "Trimonthly Field Return of Artillery Battalion 1st Army Corps."

35. Headquarters Letters Sent, vol. 185, p. 101; RG 395, entry 5850, "Return of the 2nd Brigade, 1st Division, 1st Corps, Guayama, Porto Rico July and Aug. 1898"; entry 5852, "Trimonthly Field Return U. S. Troops at Guayama, Porto Rico, August 1898," "Trimonthly Field Return Signal Corps, First Army Corps, Ponce, Porto Rico From: July 20 to September 10, 1898," "Trimonthly Field Return Artillery Battalion, 1st Army Corps, Guayama, Porto Rico August 10–20, 1898" entry 5850, "Return of Casualties: 2nd Brigade, 1st Div. 1st Corps, Guayama, P. R. on August 5, 1898," "Return of Casualties in 2nd Brigade 1st Division, 1st Corps, Guayama, P. R. 8 August 1898"; *New York Times,* August 7, 1898, p. 1 and August 9, 1989, p. 1 "Marching on San Juan."

36. Headquarters Letters Received, vol. 189, p. 74.

37. Rivero, pp. 241 ff.: *La Correspondencia,* August 23, 1898, p. 1. Reporter Richard Harding Davies later claimed to have been the first American to have entered Coamo and to have been handed the surrender by the mayor. See "The Taking of Coamo" in *The Notes of a War Correspondent* (New York, 1911), pp. 101–12.

38. "The turning movement was commenced to-day, when Gen. Brooke land- ed 8,000 men at Arroyo, sixty miles east of here. From there he can strike the mil- itary road leading to San Juan de Puerto Rico, at Cayey, beyond Abonitas [sic]. This will compel the Spanish commander, Gen. Otega [sic], who has a great rep- utation, to abandon his stronghold or be caught between two fires. It is possible that a second column may move on his left flank also, in which case the present advance on his front is only a feint" (*New York Times,* August 5, 1898, p. 1, "May Be a Fight At Abonitas"). On August 9 Gilmore advised Wilson that Brooke had received orders to proceed toward Cayey: "Should he accomplish this, it will ren- der the position at Aibonito untenable." The same day Wilson was told to obtain information about a road from Coamo to Barranquitas (Headquarters Letters Sent, vol. 185, p. 127).

39. Headquarters Letters Sent, vol. 185, pp. 73, 74, 92: Headquarters Letters Received, vol. 189, pp. 87, 88, 92, 95.

40. Rivero, pp. 296–97; Headquarters Letters Received, vol. 189, pp. 77–78, 82, 89, 96, 133.

41. "General Schwan's Report of Operations in the Campaign in Porto Rico," RG 395, entry 5857; Rivero, pp. 323–36; Herrmann, From Yauco to Las Marías.

42. See Rivero, 635. The Spanish public was greatly disappointed about the attitude of Puerto Ricans toward the invaders (see "Spaniards Feel Disheartened," *New York Times*, August 18, 1989, p. 2; "Derecho del Pataleo," *La Bomba*, September 24, 1898, p. 1).

43. "Puerto Rico an Easy Conquest," *New York Times*, August 1, 1898. On August 22 Corporal William Lang, of "K" Company, 11th Infantry Regiment, wrote from Mayagüez: "The Porto Ricans cannot do enough for us. They show their sympathy in a thousand ways. When we came through Mayagüez the women began to cry and put their arms around our necks, shouting, 'Viva America!'" (*Chicago Daily News*, September 7, 1898, p. 3). Comments such as this one, made during the weeks following the invasion, may serve to illustrate the degree of frustration that Puerto Ricans felt with the Spanish régime, and the enthusiasm with which they collaborated with the invading forces.

44. "Some people have been disposed to regard the conquest of Puerto Rico as ridiculously, if not absurdly, easy, and there is no doubt that the disposition of the inhabitants had much to do with the comfort and safety of the invaders. Spaniards are Spaniards, however, and they can fight—in a way. There is no reason to suppose that the forces under Gen. Macias paid much, or even any, attention to the cheers of the islanders or to the proclamations of village Alcaldes. They observed the adequacy of Gen. Miles preparations, and retired to Aibonito or to some other place, distant and therefore tenable. . . It's a great thing to have a reputation, and a greater one to deserve it" ("Personal," *New York Times*, August 11, 1898, p. 6.).

45. Richard Harding Davis, *The Cuban and Porto Rican Campaigns*, pp. 299–300, 305.

46. "Blundering at Porto Rico," *Chicago Daily News*, September 17, 1898, p. 4; "Starvation Prevails in 3d Illinois at Guayama, Porto Rico," ibid., September 26, 1898, p. 1; "Major Shaw is Acquitted," ibid., September 7, 1898, p. 3.

47. "Marching into Porto Rico," *The Chicago Daily News*, September 7, 1898, p. 3.

48. Sandburg, p. 418.

49. See Lewis Hanlow, Van Deusen et al., eds., *Quinquennial Record of the Class of 'Ninety-Eight of Princeton University* (Philadelphia, 1903), pp. 41–42, 49, 186.

50. Anthony Fiala, *Troop "C" in Service: An Account of the Part Played by Troop "C" of the New York Volunteer Cavalry in the Spanish-American War* (Brooklyn:1899), pp. 56–58. Fiala also describes the ineptitude that caused the

transport ship to run aground at the entrance to the port of Guánica.

51. Henry F. Keenan, *The Conflict with Spain: A History of the War Based Upon Official Reports and Descriptions of Eye-Witnesses* (Philadelphia, 1898), p. 474.

52. Crane was a reporter for *The New York Journal*. See G. J. A. O'Toole, op cit., pp. 356–57.

53. See, for example, Endwin Erle Sparks, *The Expansion of the American People: Social and Territorial* (Chicago, 1900), pp. 445–46.

54. *La Correspondencia,* June 13, 1898, p. 2.

55. NARA, RG 108, entry 122, vol. 191, p. 38.

56. Esteban López-Jiménez, "Epoca de dolor: Páginas Tristes," in "Escapes de Vapor," an unpublished volume of three autobiographical essays. I am grateful to Dr. Luce López Baralt for access to a photocopy of this invaluable testimony, written in January of 1900. About these events see also Rivero, chapter 22, "Sucesos de Fajardo."

57. "A D[on] Juan B. Nieves, Autor del Folleto 'La Anexión de Puerto Rico a E. E. U. U.', " *La Bruja*, October 22, 1898, p. 2.

58. NARA, RG 108, entry 122, vol. 191, p. 38.

59. "Ayer y Hoy," *El Combate*, Year 1, no. 55, Tuesday, July 25, 1899, p. 2.

NOTES TO CHAPTER 3

1. The San Juan press refers to residents of the capital—particularly civil servants—who escaped to live in the countryside during the war as *embriscados* [*embriscar*, according to Rubén del Rosario, *Vocabulario puertorriqueño,* 3d ed. (Río Piedras: Editorial Edil, 1980) means to flee or escape.—Tr.] (See Rivero, p. 564). In Quebradillas and other municipalities the *embriscados* were members of the armed bands, called *tiznados* elsewhere.

2. NARA, RG 108, entry 122, Army Headquarters Letters Received, vol. 190, pp. 105, 113; vol. 191, p. 20. The way events were first reported in *La Bruja*, published in Mayagüez, the Guardia Civil had accused the mayor, Sánchez, of not having enforced law and order ("De Aguada, La Verdad," August 31, 1898, p. 3.) but the report and the letters received by Miles, including a report from an agent in San Juan, show Sánchez openly fraternizing with de Funiak's detachment.

3. See "Nombramiento de una comisión para celebrar entrevista con el Mayor General Henry sobre las facultades del Ayuntamiento en sus distintos organismos. . .," AMP, Asuntos Varios, sheaf 156, box 147, dossier 183, which includes a copy of the "Memoria presentada por una comisión de este ayuntamiento al

honorable General Henry y aprobada por esta superior autoridad del distrito sobre extensión de la autonomía municipal" (Ponce, October 5, 1898).

4. See *La Bruja,* September 4, 1898, p. 2, "Fuego graneado." About the removal from office of the mayor of Adjuntas in August, 1898, see "Miscellaneous Reports" in NARA, RG 395, entry 5857.

5. See "Robo inicuo," in *La Bomba,* September 24, 1898, p. 1: "Some merchants who do business with the farmers and receive payment in harvested coffee are extending the due date on the promissory notes until March or April, at which time they they expect our currency will have been replaced by U.S. dollars, so they will be paid in American gold for what they sold for Puerto Rican pesos."

6. Puerto Rico Letters Received, vol. 8, number 1953; Mayagüez Letters Received, box 1, letter from Capt. James Buchanan to Lt. Jenkins. On October 23, 1898, *The Chicago Tribune,* under the headline "Anxious to be Clerks in Porto Rico" reported on its front page that the State Department was swamped with letters requesting jobs in Puerto Rico and Cuba. On January 24, 1899, Brigadier General Grant wrote to the Adjutant General at State, ". . . nearly every steamer from the United States brings a lot of impecunious characters to the Island who are unable to secure employment, and soon find themselves in a destitute and deplorable condition." (San Juan Letters Sent vol. 2, p. 30, number 841).

7. Letter from Antonio Orta to the Mayagüez Military Commander, NARA, RG 395, entry 5858, "Spanish Language Papers"; Headquarters Letters Sent, vol 186, p. 126.

8. See *La Correspondencia,* January 2, 1892, p. 3, and October 10, 1895, p. 3; AGPR, Ponce Superior Court, Criminal 1890–99, box xv, Audiencia de lo Criminal de Ponce, Minutas de Sentencias Dictadas. . . en Octubre, Noviembre y Diciembre" (1891) no. 337.

9. *El País,* May 30, 1898, p. 2; *La Unión,* July 9, 1898, p. 3.

10. AMP, sheaf 157, box 148 A, dossier 112, "Manifestación de la Presidencia respecto a que se concedan gratis toda clase de reparaciones de casas por término de seis meses a fin de dar trabajo a la clase obrera."

11. *La Correspondencia,* June 13, 1898, p. 3.

12. *New York Times,* July 27, 1898, p. 1.

13. NARA, RG108, entry 122, Headquarters Letters Received, vol. 189, p. 61, Henry to Adjutant General.

14. Ponce Letters Sent, vol. 1, p. 158. Decisive proof does not exist that the photograph of an armed band with the flag of Puerto Rico taken somewhere in the south coast depicts Aguila Blanca's band. This attribution originates in the

1899 publication of *Our Islands and Their People* (vol. 1, p. 362) and is due to efforts made—in the above and other publications of the times—to cast Cuban and Puerto Rican partisans as bandits, as part of an effort to justify the annexation of both Antillean islands. What is odd is that this allegation has been repeated without corroboration, and that Aguila Blanca has been described as holding certain political beliefs which were never ascribed to him by either Puerto Rican or American contemporary sources. See Ponce Letters Sent, vol. 1, pp. 135 ff.

15. Headquarters Letters Received, vol. 189, p. 77. The author of the message [reproduced here in the original English—Tr.] is listed as "E. Sugoring." The premature occupation of San Germán led to the return of the Spanish troops, who abandoned the city as Schwann's troops approached. In the report filed by Schwann about his activities in the western part of the island, he mentions the cooperation of *criollo* auxiliary troops.

16. See Julio Tomás Martínez-Mirabal, *Colección Martínez: Crónicas íntimas* (Arecibo, 1946); Headquarters Letters Received, vol. 189., pp. 87, 95, 98, 118.

17. AGPR, TSA, Criminal, Utuado, box 957, "Juzgado de instrucción de Utuado, Sumario 423 1898 Contra Don Salvador Pérez-Gerena y Don Ramón Hernández-Olivencia por Estafa." In 1900, Salvador Pérez-Gerena owned 40 *cuerdas* in Barrio Angeles and Ramón Hernández-Olivencia owned 18 and a half.

18. On August 9, 1898, 2nd Lt. W. H. Paine, of the 2nd Cavalry Regiment, submitted an official report about this armed band to General Stone. See Headquarters Letters Received, vol. 190, p. 35.

19. Juan Manuel Delgado has written a book on this subject, *El levantamiento de Ciales* (Río Piedras, 1980). The letter from Figueroa to Miles quoted below, however, points towards a different interpretation of the "Sucesos de Ciales," as the press of the times used to refer to the case.

20. See Headquarters Letters Received, vol. 190, pp. 63, 77, 80, 92–93; vol. 191, p. 39; vol. 186, p. 54; *La Bruja*, October 19, 1898, p. 3, "Sucesos de Ciales."

21. Headquarters Letters Received, vol. 190, p. 77. See also B. Vélez, "Los Sucesos de Ciales," *Boletín Histórico de Puerto Rico* 6 (1919), pp. 80–85. Rodulfo Figueroa was in jail under suspicion of having been involved in the burning of the property of a peninsular Spaniard, Francisco Martín, and the fire at Caserío de Coto in Ponce. General Henry freed him early in December, 1898. At the beginning of January, 1899, Figueroa was named chief of police of Juana Díaz. In this capacity he cooperated in the arrest and trial of the members of an armed band that operated around Ciales and Jayuya. (*Correo de Puerto Rico*, December 9, 1898, p. 2, and January 5, 1899, p. 3; NARA, RG 153, box 2969, dossier 11182).

22. Esperanza Mayol, *Islas*, 133–34.

23. NARA, RG 395, entry 5858, "Al General Schwann Jefe de las fuerzas americanas que operan en Mayagüez E. U."

24. Ibid. "Miscellaneous Letters," letters from Maricao's mayor Lignet to Colonel De Russy; Puerto Rico Letters Received, vol. 9, no. 2024.

25. *New York Times*, August 1, 1898, p. 1, "Puerto Rico an easy conquest." The following day the *Times* reported that instances of vandalism and revenge had taken place in other villages in the district of Ponce ("Another Town in Puerto Rico Ours," p. 1).

26. *New York Times*, August 1, 1898, p. 1, "Henry Found No Spaniards."

27. *La Correspondencia*, August 8, 1898, p. 2.

28. *La Correspondencia*, August 19, 1898, p. 2, "Noticias." About the case of an armed band in Barrio Altocuerpo Arriba, Villalba, in Juana Díaz, on August 2, 1898, see NARA, RG 153, box 2959, dossier 10780.

29. NARA, RG 396, entry 5857, "Proceedings of a Military Commission which Convened at Ponce, Porto Rico, pursuant to. . . Special Field Order number 29."

30. *La Correspondencia*, August 30, 1898, p. 1.

31. AGPR, TSA, Criminal, Utuado, box 957, dossier 266.

32. Interview with *doña* Carmen Bauzá González, daughter of the Majorcan landowner Miguel Bauzá, November 9, 1986, in Río Piedras.

33. See Esperanza Mayol, 129.

34. See Edwards, op. cit., 233 ff.; *El País*, p. 3, "De la Isla"; Headquarters Letters Received, vol. 190, p. 17 letter from José González-Hernández, mayor of San Sebastián, to the military authorities, October 11, 1898 (NARA, RG 395, entry 5858, "Miscellaneous Letters").

35. See "El Legado," in *La Bomba*, September 29, 1898, p. 2; "Crónica," in *La Bruja*, October 16, 1898, p. 1. [See also Fernando Picó, *Historia general de Puerto Rico* (Río Piedras, Ediciones Huracán, 1986), p. 215—Tr.].

36. TSA, Criminal, Utuado, box 959, lawsuit no. 260.

37. AGPR, Justicia, Confinados, box 89C, no. 504, Penal history of the mulatto prisoner Aniceto Orta y Arocho.

38. TSA, Criminal, Utuado, box 957, indictment no. 266.

39. Towards 1894 Pedro Castro-González owned two tracts of land in Viví Arriba. One measured 19 *cuerdas* and the other 15, with a total of six *cuerdas* planted in coffee. The name of one of the farms was "Covadonga," which suggests Castro might have been a native of Asturias. By 1900, however, he was paying taxes for 214 *cuerdas* in the same barrio (CFRU numbers 258 and 263; 1900 Census, 10v).

40. TSA, Criminal, Utuado, box 958, dossier 270.

41. Ramón Morel Campos, *El Porvenir de Utuado* (Ponce, 1897) pp. 118–20.

42. In 1900 Gaspar Homar owned 40 *cuerdas* in Jayuya Arriba (1900 Census, 16r).

43. TSA, Criminal, Utuado, box 959, indictment no. 280.

44. TSA, Civil, Utuado, box 271, indictment no. 3 of the Utuado Municipal Courthouse and no. 391 of the Arecibo Justice Court; 1900 Census, 5v. Apparently this case was heard by the Provisional Federal Court; I am unaware of the outcome.

45. TSA, Criminal, Utuado, Box 959, dossier 282, 1900 Census, 4 v.

46. Regarding this group see TSA, Criminal, Utuado, box 965, dossier 442. Pablo Ferri, an illiterate, was still in jail awaiting trial in May, 1899, when Lino Guzmán wrote a letter in his name to the military commander in Mayagüez requesting that "work be assigned to me so that with the money they might wish to give me I may purchase a change of clothes" (Mayagüez Letters Received, box 1, no. 614). "La Mano Negra" was a popular name for anarchical rural groups in Andalusia toward the end of the 19th century. See Clara E. Lido, "Agrarian Anarchism in Andalusia: Documents on the Mano Negra," *International Review of Social History*, 14 (1969), 315–52; Temma Kaplan, *Anarchists of Andalusia, 1868–1903* (Princeton: Princeton University Press, 1977).

47. NARA, RG 153, box 2969, dossier 11,175.

48. In 1900 Rafael Herrera owned 75 *cuerdas* in Don Alonso (1900 Census, 12v).

49. TSA, Criminal, Utuado, box 959, dossier 289.

50. TSA, Criminal, Utuado, box 958, dossier 301.

51. TSA, Criminal, Utuado, box 958, dossier 306.

52. TSA, Criminal, Utuado, box 958, dossier 307.

53. RG 395, entry 5957, "Proceedings of a Military Commission. . ."; Puerto Rico Letters Received, vol. 2, no. 253–54; see Fiala, op. cit. 88. Rigau and Lanzo were acquitted.

54. *La Correspondencia*, August 23, 1898, p. 1; August 31, p. 2.

55. *El País*, October 7, 1898, p. 3.

56. Headquarters Letters Sent, vol. 187, p. 42.

57. San Juan Letters Sent, vol. 1, pp. 88–89.

58. Thomas Sherman, S. J., "A Month in Porto Rico," *Messenger of the Sacred Heart* 33 (1898), 1078–79. I am grateful to my fellow Jesuit Manuel Maza for sending a photocopy of this article. Blanco started by acquiring 80 *cuerdas* in 1890. Towards 1896, his hacienda measured 400 *cuerdas*, of which 260 would produce the coffee harvest. At the time, the hacienda was equipped with a double warehouse with 20 movable drying trays, another warehouse with ten, a wood

storage shed, another building with an oxen-powered mill, a building that housed machinery, tanks for washing coffee berries, a family residence, an overseer's office, a paved area used for drying coffee in the sun, a cistern, and 32 houses for workers. By 1900 Blanco's property measured 522 *cuerdas* (Morel Campos, *Porvenir*, 146–47; CFRU numbers 116 and 118; 1900 Census, 6 r).

59. For example, on the 24th of September Judge Félix Santoni, of Utuado, wrote a letter to the Mayagüez District Court to report that he was disqualifying himself from hearing the case in which Eusebio Pérez-Grau had been the victim of a band of robbers, because it fell under military jurisdiction (TSA, Criminal, Utuado, box 959, dossier 260, 1 r).

NOTES TO CHAPTER FOUR

1. "At twelve today, the American flag was raised at the old city hall as a sign that Spanish sovereignty had ended in Puerto Rico, and American sovereignty began. A detachment of soldiers was at the center of the main plaza to do the honor, and cannon shots were fired from the fortresses and war ships. Around the plaza, on sidewalks, and on some balconies, there were few people seriously witnessing the ceremony of the changing of the flags. Afterwards, soldiers and onlookers went away in the midst of the most imposing silence" ("Cambio de estrella," *El País* 18 Oct. 1898: 2). See "Porto Rico Comes under the Stars and Stripes to-day and comes to stay," *Chicago Daily News* 18 Oct. 1898: 4; "Flag is Raised over San Juan," *Chicago Tribune* 19 Oct. 1898: 12.

2. Beisner, op. cit. "Mr. Hoar on Imperialism," *New York Times* 30 July 1898: 1; "Fears an Imperial Policy Ex-Attorney General Harmon Sees Grave Danger in Territorial Acquisitions," ibid., 13 July 1898: 7; "Opposed to Annexation," ibid.: 2; "Herbert Not For Expansion," *Chicago Daily News* 19 Oct. 1898: 11; "Against Holding the Islands," *New York Tribune* 3 Nov. 1898: 7. On the other hand, the *Kansas City Star* saw in the conquests a way out "for that restless element which has caused most of the troubles in the industrial world, and would furnish the means to gratify the spirit of adventure which is unconquerable in the American nature" (quoted in the *New York Herald* 20 Dec. 1898: 8).

3. "Congress Adjourns Exciting Scenes Mark the Close in the House Patriotic Songs Are Sung," *New York Times* 9 July 1898: 4.

4. On these subjects, see Edward J. Berbusse, S.J., *The United States in Puerto Rico, 1898–1900* (Chapel Hill: University of North Carolina Press, 1966); Lyman J. Gould, *La Ley Foraker: Raíces de la política colonial de los Estados Unidos,* trans. Jorge Luis Morales (Río Piedras: University of Puerto Rico Press, 1969), orig: *The Foraker Act: The Roots of American Colonial Policy* (Ann

Arbor, Mich.: University Microfilms, 1958); María Dolores Luque de Sánchez, *La ocupación norteamericana y la Ley Foraker* (Río Piedras: University of Puerto Rico Press, 1980); Carmen I. Raffucci, *El gobierno civil y la Ley Foraker* (Río Piedras: University of Puerto Rico Press, 1981).

5. See "Noticias," *El País* 27 May 1898: 2, about the limiting of credit to Aibonito farmers in Cayey and Coamo.

6. TSA, Criminal, Utuado, box 961, indictment 349, 6 r.

7. TSA, Criminal, Utuado, box 958, case 382, 8 r.

8. TSA, Criminal, Utuado, box 963, dossier 414, I v.

9. TSA, Criminal, Utuado, box 959, dossier 303.

10. Vicente Bernacet came to Utuado in 1883. With a down payment of 250 pesos he bought land, at Caonillas Abajo, on installments. At first he had only one farm worker. Coffee was processed in Arecibo. By 1896, his Hacienda Pandura was made up of 1,200 cuerdas, 100 of which were used in the production of coffee. Besides coffee, he sold timber, minor crops, medicinal plants, fruit, honey and livestock [Morel Campos, "Porvenir de Utuado," 150–53; CFRU nos. 108, 109, 110; Padrón 1900, 6 r.].

11. TSA, Criminal, Utuado, box 964, dossier 398.

12. TSA, Criminal, Utuado, box 964, dossier 402.

13. TSA, Criminal, Utuado, box 965, indictment no. 438.

14. For example, Pedro Monserrate Segarra was arrested for buying coffee supposedly stolen from the Gandarilla succession in Lares. Segarra was able to prove he had bought it before the warehouse on that farm was looted by a band (TSA, Criminal, Utuado, box 957, dossier 419). See also NARA, RG 153, box 2969, dossier 11182, testimony of Police Captain Pedro Guerrero about the stealing of coffee from José Fuster; and the instructions from the assistant adjutant general of San Juan to the commanders in the North about some coffee stolen in Utuado and carried in marked bags that could be detected: "They may market coffee in your place" (San Juan Letters Sent, vol. 1, pp. 91–92).

15. TSA, Criminal, Utuado, box 962, "Criminal, Año 1898 Sumario núm. 430, Delito Robo Perjudicado Juan Ginard," 7 r–8 v.

16. TSA, Criminal, Utuado, box 961, indictment no. 349, 19 r.

17. NARA, RG 153, box 2944, dossier 10219, p. 10: "Q. What became of Arbona's account books? A. Bautista González ordered that the books should be taken out of my trunk, and then I told them that if any harm came to those books he could not collect anything. They asked me if I had any account with the house, and I answered that there was only 27 cents of the money there that belonged to me, and then this Mr. Gonzalez took out 27 cents out of his pocket and gave it to me. This Mr. Gonzalez delivered the books to Pedro Vargas for him to burn. Then

Pedro Vargas took a long sabre and cut them in two and threw them into a decalitro and poured kerosene on them and set fire to them. After they had burned, with the same sabre he gave a cut at the decalitro and threw it out into the field."

18. TSA, Criminal, Utuado, box 964, indictment no. 411, 6v–7r; *El País* 18 Oct. 1898: 3.

19. NARA, RG 153, box 2944, dossier 10219, p. 10.

20. NARA, RG 395, San Juan Letters Sent, vol. 2, no. 835, p. 25.

21. San Juan Letters Sent, vol. 1, p. 252, and vol. 2, pp. 196–97; Aguadilla Letters Sent, vol. 2, p. 1 A; Aguadilla Letters Received, telegram 37; Mayagüez Letters Sent, vol. 1, no. 21, p. 47; Puerto Rico Letters Received, vol. 3, no. 552. *El Territorio* 28 Mar. 1899: 3; *El Correo de Puerto Rico* 14 Dec. 1898: 3.

22. *El Correo de Puerto Rico* 6 Dec. 1898: 2–3.

23. *El Correo de Puerto Rico* 18 Jan. 1899: 3.

24. "The boys were released by the civil judge, which was contrary to instructions conveyed to him, according to what I understood to be the wishes of the Commanding General, viz., That the boys should be kept until frightened into telling who had incited them to start the fires in the sugar cane fields" (San Juan Letters Sent, vol. 2, no. 835, p. 27).

25. *El Correo de Puerto Rico* 22 Jan. 1899: 3.

26. Aguadilla Letters Sent, vol. 1, no. 4, p. 708; *El Boletín Mercantil* 13 Feb. 1899: 4; 21 Mar.: 2.

27. On the case of Mano Negra in Adjuntas, see TSA, Criminal, Utuado, box 965, dossier 442.

28. NARA, RG 153, box 2944, dossiers 10215, 10224; box 2969, dossiers 11172, 11174.

29. Ibid., box 2944, dossier 10224; box 2969, dossier 11172.

30. See Blanca Silvestrini, *Violencia y criminalidad en Puerto Rico, 1898–1973* (Río Piedras: University of Puerto Rico Press, 1980) 23ss.; Pedro A. Vales, Astrid A. Ortiz and Noel E. Mattei, *Patrones de criminalidad en Puerto Rico: Apreciación socio-histórica: 1898–1980* (Río Piedras: n.p., 1982) 73ss.

31. *El Correo de Puerto Rico* 26 Oct. 1898: 2.

32. *El Vesuvius* 29 Oct. 1898: 4; *San Juan News* 30 and 31 Dec. 1899: 1.

33. Jacobo Córdova Chirino, *Los que murieron en la horca* (San Juan: Cordillera, 1975) 33–46.

34. TSA, Criminal, Utuado, box 965, "Sumario núm. 443 de 1898, Rollo núm. 1979 de 1898. Robo a D. Guillermo Rullan."

35. See TSA, Criminal, Utuado, box 969, "Tribunal de Justicia del Distrito de Arecibo, Rollo núm. 363, Año 1899, Juzgado Municipal de Utuado, Asesinato de D. Claudio Mora."

36. *La Bruja* 31 Aug. 1898: 2–3. A rural police was created in Ponce in November (AMP, Asuntos Varios, docket 158, dossier 266).

37. NARA, R G 395, entry 5908, Mayagüez Letters Received, box 1. Letter dated January 8, 1899, from the commander in Las Marías to his superior in Mayagüez.

38. TSA, Criminal, Utuado, box 966, "Criminal Año 1898 Sumario no. 482 Delito Lesiones Menos Graves Perjudicado D. Antonino García Procesado José Cuevas Montalvo. Juzgado de Instrucción de Utuado," 12 v–14 r.

39. Ibid., 2 r.

40. San Juan Letters Sent, vol. 2, pp. 124–26.

41. "Noticias Generales," *La Democracia* 16 May 1899: 3. Henry's order was amended by Davis "in the sense that the eight hours of work a day mentioned . . . are valid only for service contracts in which a specific salary has been agreed to, and without detriment to agreements between the parties increasing or decreasing said term" (*La Democracia* 18 May: 3). This modification effectively cut back on the progress achieved, because it authorized employers to "agree" to work days of traditional length. On May 26, *La Democracia* reported "the issue of eight hours has caused Carolina workers to go on strike" (p. 3).

42. AMP, Asuntos Varios, docket 163, dossier 149, "1899. Trabajos de propaganda realizados en este término municipal por Don Ramón Morell Campos." In January of the same year, Morell Campos had given public speeches at the Liga Obrera in Ponce about the "general character of deficient socialist schools," "political economy," "capital and work, the concept of accumulation," and "commentaries on the works of Samuel Smiles, character, saving, and 'Help yourself'" (*El Correo de Puerto Rico* 4 Jan. 1899: 3).

43. *La Estrella Solitaria* 4 Oct. 1898: 2.

44. "Tristezas y alegrías," *El País* 15 Oct. 1898: 2–3.

45. NARA, RG 395, Puerto Rico Letters Received, vol. 5, no. 1123.

46. *New York Daily Tribune* 29 Nov. 1898: 2.

47. Puerto Rico Letters Received, vol. 5, no. 1123, pp. 2–3.

48. San Juan Letters Sent, vol. 1, no. 433, p. 158.

49. Puerto Rico Letters Received, vol. 3, no. 552; San Juan Letters Sent, vol. 1, no. 433, p. 159; vol. 2, no. 851, p. 64.

50. Ibid., vol. 1, pp. 134, 140, 185; vol. 2, no. 835, p. 28; Vieques Letters Received 1899, no. 7, p. 2; Mayagüez Letters Received, box 6, letter from the assistant to the assistant adjutant general in Ponce to the commander in Mayagüez; RG 395, entry 5849, "Post Return of Company G 47th N.Y. V. Infantry for the Month of December, 1898; Station: Carolina. Record of Events." The answer to the commander in Toa Alta about the midnight mass was that there

was no order to stop its being held, "but people must not be allowed to take advantage of this celebration to disguise themselves and commit depredation."

NOTES TO CHAPTER 5

1. *La Correspondencia de Puerto Rico* 23 Aug. 1898: 2.

2. See Thomas E. Sherman, "A Month in Porto Rico," *The Messenger of the Sacred Heart* 33 (1898): 1078–79.

3. NARA, RG 395, entry 5852, Field Returns, "Trimonthly Field Return District of Ponce, Porto Rico From: Sept. 10 to October 20, 1898, Record of Events": "Sergt. T.T. Edwards Co. A, 1st Ky. Vol. Infantry, stationed near Utuado, in repelling a band of bandits, killed the leader, and wounded two others;" Headquarters Letters Received, vol. 190, p. 94.

4. See, for example, "Anarchy in Porto Rico. Robbery and Arson Committed by Brigands," *New York Tribune* 1 Nov. 1898: 1.

5. Puerto Rico Letters Received, vol. 2, no. 310; RG 153, box 2944, dossier 10216.

6. Mayagüez Letters Sent, vol. 1, p. 14.

7. *Special Orders 1898*, no. 52, par. 1, 2, 3. The Arecibo commission was created by *Special Order* no. 39, par. 7, of February 16, 1899.

8. NARA, RG 153, box 2937, dossier 9926; Confinados, box 89, dossier 4645.

9. Juan Terreforte, "Por los Presos," *El Combate* 19 Sept. 1899: 1.

10. For example, when Henry approved Carlos Santos Centeno's pardon, accused of wounding a soldier of the 19th Infantry Regiment in the course of a fight in Yauco, Henry said the case provided "an illustration of the humanity and beneficence of the law as administered by American Military Tribunals, it being their purpose to secure a speedy trial, to ascertain the exact truth, and where the guilt of the accused is established beyond a reasonable doubt, to mete out punishment for the protection of society" (*Special Orders* no. 31, par. 10, February 7, 1899).

11. RG 153, box 2944, dossier 10219, p. 38.

12. NARA, RG 153, box 2969, dossier 11176.

13. On this subject see Eric J. Hobsbawm, *Primitive Rebels: Studies in Archaic Forms of Social Movements in the 19th and 20th Centuries* (Manchester: Manchester University Press, 1959), and María Poumier-Taquechel, *Contribution a l'étude du banditisme social a Cuba: L'histoire de Manuel Garcia "Rey de los Campos de Cuba" (1851–1895)* (Lille: n.p., 1986). On White Eagle, in popular literature see "Breve historia de José Maldonado, alias 'White Eagle,' Noble

Hijo de Villalba, Defensor de la Independiencia de Puerto Rico," in "La Literatura popular," *La Revista del Centro de Estudios Avanzados de Puerto Rico y el Caribe* 1 (1985): 41.

14. "Los sucesos de ayer," *La Democracia* 17 May 1898: 2: Confinados 89 A, dossier 451, copy of the sentence for stealing of Eduvijis Vázquez Paduanes and others in 1896.

15. Headquarters Letters Received, vol. 190, p. 82.

16. Puerto Rico Letters Received, vol. 8, no. 1882.

17. *El Correo de Puerto Rico* 26, 27 and 28 Dec. 1898: 3.

18. "Maldonado is free, and when he visited the offices of El Correo yesterday people crowded at the doors of the establishment to see him," "Pepe Maldonado," *El Correo de Puerto Rico* 5 Jan. 1899: 2. *La Correspondencia* criticized the pardon (quoted in "Agresión?," *El Correo* 18 Jan.: 2).

19. Ponce Letters Sent, vol. 1, pp. 157–66; *La Democracia* and *El Combate*, existing numbers for May and June 1899.

20. William S. Bryan, ed., *Our Islands and Their People* (St. Louis, New York, etc.: N.D. Thompson, 1899), vol. 1, p. 362. Most probably, the photograph corresponds to a group under [the leadership] of Mattei Lluveras, Mateo Fajardo or Lugo Viñas.

NOTES TO CHAPTER 6

1. See Robert M. Utley, *Frontier Regulars: The United States Army and the Indian 1866–1891* (New York: n.p., 1973) 153–54, 276 ss.

2. When it was attempted to separate the Bureau of Insular Affairs from the War Department in 1920, the argument used by Secretary of War Newton Baker to oppose it was that the privileged knowledge of the then General McIntyre would be lost (Truman R. Clark, *Puerto Rico and the United States, 1917–1933* (Pittsburgh: University of Pittsburgh P, 1975) 27–28).

3. Army Register.

4. Aguadilla Letters Sent, vol. 2, p. 42.

5. Ponce Letters Sent, vol. 1, p. 117.

6. Mayagüez Letters Received, box 1, correspondence between Lieutenant De Funiak and Colonel Carr, August to November 1899.

7. Headquarters Letters Sent, vol. 186, p. 126; RG 395, entry 5858, "Spanish Language Papers," letter from Orta; San Juan Letters Sent, vol. 1, p. 140; Vieques Letters Received, no. 42, p. 13.

8. NARA, RG 395, entry 5858, "Spanish Language Papers," letter to Santiago R. Palmer, ineligible signature.

9. Yauco Letters Received, vol. 1, p. 59.

10. NARA, RG 153, box 2944, dossier 10214, p. 31; dossier 10219, pp. 15–16.

11. Edwards, p. 112.

12. "Natives Eager to Aid Miles," *New York Times* 1 Aug. 1898: 1; "Marching in Porto Rico," *Chicago Daily News* 7 Sept. 1898: 3; Socorro Girón, op. cit., pp. 359–60, letter from sailor Henry Williams to his father. Herrmann and Edwards, in their respective works, published later, manifested reservations about the cordiality of "the natives." For Herrmann, "A Chinese host would have been received with just as much acclaim as we were, had they come as conquering heroes." He recommended to the Americans to trust only the educated class, of pure Spanish blood. He thought that part of the masses was "ignorant, filthy, untruthful, lazy, treacherous, murderous, brutal and black" (op. cit., pp. 34–35 and 68). To Edwards, "the enthusiastic reception accorded the troops on all sides in the country and by the crowds in the streets was the expression not of the substantial class of the island but of the crowds always foremost on such occasions in expressing the spirit of the mob . . . and while it is of course pleasant to receive a welcome even from the irresponsible class, it is not safe to allow that to stand as the expression of the minds of the intelligent natives" (op. cit., p. 109).

13. See, for example, the court martial of Corporal Thomas O'Donnel, from K Company of the 19th Infantry (for causing a disturbance in the store of Genaro López in Ponce, and having threatened him with a revolver for not selling him liquor; RG 153, box 2937, dossier 9924). The repeated disturbances created by members of the 5th Cavalry in Mayagüez is described in detail in the Mayagüez Summary Court, vol. 2 (RG 395, entry 5916).

14. The first case I found was the claim of Teodoro Santiago Colón, on August 16, for damage to a palisade on his Coamo property done by soldiers who were looking for firewood to use in cooking. (RG 395, entry 5857, letter to Major General Wilson.) In the following months, several property owners made claims to the military government for damages caused by military operations on July and August 1898, and for the individual action of soldiers.

15. NARA, RG 395, entry 5858, "Spanish Language Papers."

16. TSA, Criminal, Utuado, box 968, indictment no. 29; Francisco Ramos, *Viejo rincón utuadeño* (Utuado: Farmacia Central Utuado, 1946) 161; Vieques Letters Received, no. 81, p. 25, photocopy of a copy of the minutes of the Utuado municipal government, dated March 27, 1899, given to me by Atty. Alfonso García Martínez, grandchild of Mayor Ramiro Martínez.

17. See *La Democracia* 22 Feb. 1899: 2.

18. See San Juan Letters Sent, vol. 2, no. 1054, p. 102; no. 1113, pp. 122–23;

RG 153, box 2969, dossier 11176; *Special Orders*, no. 114, par. 1. See case of Luis Aponte in RG 153, box 2959, dossier 10775.

19. Mayagüez Letters Received, box 1, letter dated December 25, 1898, from the commander in Las Marías, Lieutenant Elliott, to the colonel commander of the Mayagüez military district.

20. NARA, RG 395, entry 5857.

21. Puerto Rico Letters Received, vol. 8, no. 1849; San Juan Letters Sent, vol. 1, nos. 453–54, p. 166.

22. Ibid., no. 284; Puerto Rico Letters Received, vol. 6, no. 1384.

23. "overbearing in his treatment of natives," Arecibo Letters Sent, no. 152, pp. 105–6.

24. San Juan Letters Sent, vol. 2, p. 26.

25. *El Territorio* 18 July 1899: 3. Ponce Letters Sent, pp. 185–86; RG 395, entry 5849, "Post Return of Ponce, Puerto Rico, Commanded by Major Alfred L. Myer, 11th Infantry, for the Month of June, 1899."

26. *El Territorio* 11 Dec. 1899: 3.

27. *La Estrella Solitaria* 4 Oct. 1898: 3. *El Combate* and *La Democracia*, in Ponce, and *La Bruja*, in Mayagüez, also made strong claims to the military commanders. The ruling class resented the soldiers' invasion of the spaces until then reserved tacitly for them, and the soldiers bringing with them the "ladies of the night." Both in Ponce and Mayagüez, before 1898, prostitution was regulated and limited to specific wards.

28. NARA, RG 395, entry 5857, report from Captain Francis W. Mansfield: "Report of investigation on Isabella affair."

29. Arecibo Letters Sent 1899–1900, no. 32, p. 17; RG 395, entry 5858. "Letters Received Aibonito 1899," letter from Adjutant General Hall to Captain Wheeler about military discipline in Aibonito, April 7, 1899.

30. See B. López, "Viaje al extranjero De la Capital a Ponce Primera jornada," *La Correspondencia* 23 Aug. 1898. Sandburg recalled considering his captain, Thomas Leslie McGirr, a lawyer from his home town, arrogant because although elected by the soldiers he did not fraternize with them (Carl Sandburg, *Always the Young Strangers* (New York: Harcourt, 1953) 404 and 422).

31. NARA, RG 153, box 2969, dossier 11164.

32. Ibid., box 2974, dossier 11393.

33. Puerto Rico Letters Received, vol. 7, no. 1531.

34. Aguadilla Letters Sent, vol. 1, pp. 159–61; vol. 2, pp. 37–46; Lares Letters Sent, no. 46, p. 54; Ponce Letters Sent, vol. 2, pp. 90–93; San Juan Letters Sent, vol. 2, pp. 202–207; Yauco Letters Sent, no. 112, p. 114.

35. Ponce Letters Received 1898–99, no. 760, p. 237 and no. 1041, p. 267;

Yauco Letters Received, vol. 1, no. 108, p. 123; Yauco Letters Sent, no. 2, p. 49; *El Territorio* 16 Mar. 1899: 3, "Aguadilla merchants complain about the provision that forces them to close their establishments on Sundays, since this measure harms their interests." In Yauco, however, it was the store clerks who asked the military authorities to close the stores on Sundays ("De Yauco," *El Correo de Puerto Rico* 25 Oct. 1898: 2).

36. *Boletín Mercantil* 1 Apr. 1899: 2; Mayagüez Letters Sent, vol. 2, no. 148, p. 30; Mayagüez Letters Received, box 1, correspondence between Lieutenant Colonel Carr and the adjutant general, started on May 21, 1899.

37. On this subject, see Blanca Silvestrini, "La política de salud pública de los Estados Unidos en Puerto Rico, 1898–1913," *Politics, Society and Culture in the Caribbean*, (San Juan: University of Puerto Rico, 1983) 67–83.

38. Aibonito Letters Sent, vol. 1, no. 94, pp. 50–52. The mayor blamed the interpreter (ibid., p. 56).

39. Captain Vernou, in Yauco, to the adjutant general in Ponce, March 6, 1899 (Yauco Letters Sent, no. 68, p. 85). See also RG 395, entry 5875, Aguadilla Letters Received, telegrams 19 and 23; Mayagüez Letters Received, box 1, letter from Carmen Rodríguez de Román to Colonel Carr.

40. Headquarters Letters Sent, vol. 187, p. 59; RG 395, entry 5875, Aguadilla Letters Received, telegram from Lieutenant Gregg in Isabela to Captain Mansfield in Aguadilla, December 6, 1898; Yauco Letters Sent, pp. 59, 61, 71, 72; *El País* 11 Oct. 1898: 3. On November 22, 1898, an American, A.N.A. Johnson offered to sell yokes to substitute for goads to the Ponce municipal government. He presented in support of his offer a letter from Assistant Adjutant General Cassatt, with Henry's endorsement. However, the Ponce municipal government did not take the bait, "considering that the intention of the solicitor is purely private; it is for speculation and the Municipality does not have any part in it" (AMP, docket 157, dossier 284).

41. Lares Letters Sent, no. 2, p. 49; Yauco Letters Sent, no. 46, p. 71 bis; no. 79, pp. 96–98; no. 117, p. 118.

42. Mayagüez Letter Received, box 1, letter dated January 17, from the secretary of justice to General Henry.

43. Headquarters Letters Sent, vol. 186; pp. 108 and 130; Headquarters Letters Received, vol. 190, p. 129; *La Correspondencia de Puerto Rico* 23 Aug. 1898: 2.

44. See "Las cosas de Mr. Henry," *El Combate* 10 June 1899: 2.

45. Ponce Letters Received 1898–99, no. 1161, p. 80, and no. 1985, p. 155 ; Mayagüez Letters Sent, vol. 1, p. 13; Puerto Rico Letters Received, vol. 7, no. 1636; General Orders 1899, no. 26; "Plans Reform for Porto Rico," *New York*

Herald 24 Dec. 1898: 5.

46. Yauco Letters Sent, pp. 84–85, 93–94, 112 and 120.

47. Mayagüez Letters Sent, vol. 1, pp. 86–87; *El Territorio* 15 Mar. 1899: 3.

48. *El Combate* 13 June 1899: 2.

49. See Victor M. Gil de Rubio, *Periodismo patriótico de Evaristo Izcoa Díaz (Biografía)* (San Juan: Liga de Coop. de PR, 1977); *El Territorio* 11 Dec. 1899: 2.

50. *El Imparcial* 29 Dec. 1899: 2.

51. Puerto Rico Letters Received, vol. 3, no. 696; San Juan Letters Sent, vol. 1, no. 551 and no. 552, p. 197; no. 556, p. 198; no. 564, p. 200.

52. Adjuntas Letters Sent 1899–1900, no. 12, p. 5 and no. 19, p. 9; RG 395, entry 5858, "Letters Received Aibonito 1899," report from soldier R.M. Parker about the destruction in Aguas Buenas, report of the military doctor Herbert McCanathy about the devastation in Comerío, and report from Corporal Frederick Anderson about the losses on Barros (Orocovis); Aibonito Letters Sent, vol. 1, pp. 60–62; Arecibo Letters Sent 1899–1900, no. 72, pp. 39–41; no. 73, pp. 42–52; RG 395, entry 5849, "Post Return of 5th Cavalry Troop C for August 1899 Humacao"; Lares Letters Sent, no. 20, pp. 37–38 and no. 28, p. 42; RG 395, entry 5875, Aguadilla Letters Received, letter from Mayor Juan C. Sánchez of Moca to the military commander in Aguadilla; Ponce Letters Sent, vol. 1, no. 404, pp. 235–41; no. 405, pp. 241–42; no. 411, pp. 244–48; vol. 2, no. 605, pp. 63–65.

53. See NARA, RG 395, entry 5858, "Letters Received San German, P. R. 1899–1900," correspondence about the aid after the hurricane.

54. *El Combate* 6 Sept. 1899: 3; Lares Letters Sent, no. 39, p. 50; AGPR, Fondo del Tribunal Superior de Ponce, Criminal 1890–99, box XV, "Diligencias sumarias preventivas instruidas en virtud de querella formulada por Don Vicente Rodríguez contra Alejandro Rivera Pagán, y sus hijos Primitivo, Acisclo y Pedro Rivera y Rivera por robo incendio y asesinato de Don Domingo Ricci, su esposa e hijo ocurrido en el mes de Febrero de 1900."

55. The advertisements of Scott's Emulsion used to quote the testimony of eminent doctors. At least on two occasions their advertisements quoted "Doctor Ramón Emeterio Betances, Puerto Rican doctor, living in Paris." It is a sad irony that he was not allowed to publish in his country's press but was shown advertising "an excellent medicine that renders the best results on those illnesses in which simple cod liver has been prescribed" (*La Correspondencia de Puerto Rico* 31 Oct. 1895: 3; *El País* 31 Jan. 1898: 3).

56. On January 31, 1898, "Kelly Slider" reported in *El País* a game of "baseball . . . of nine complete innings," in the Velódromo, between the Almendares

and Borinquen teams.

57. Ponce Letters Received 1898–99, no. 234, p. 18.

58. *El País* 5 Oct. 1898: 3; *La Bruja* 17 Aug. 1898: 2.

59. *El Combate* 18 Sept. 1899: 1.

60. *El País* 17 Feb. 1899: 3.

61. See Sherman, loc. cit., 1076.

62. See "Fuego Graneado," *La Bruja* 4 Sept. 1898: 2; Samuel Silva Gotay, "La Iglesia Protestante como agente de americanización en Puerto Rico," in Blanca Silvestrini, ed., *Politics, Society and Culture in the Caribbean* (San Juan: University of Puerto Rico, 1983), 39–66.

63. The issue of the flags began with a journalist who commented, several days after the invasion, that the only failure of Miles had been not having foreseen the huge demand of the Puerto Ricans for American flags. The Lafayette veterans' club in New York notified the secretary of war, and he in turn notified Miles' assistant, Gilmore, that the club would provide flags to all public schools in Puerto Rico. On August 8, General Gilmore answered that there were 546 public schools and 38 private schools on the island (Headquarters Letters Received, vol. 189, p. 127; Headquarters Letters Sent, vol. 185, p. 115).

64. Yauco Letters Sent, no. 35, pp. 47–48.

65. For example, Lieutenant Seaborn Chiles, of the 11th Infantry, military commander in Aguadilla in 1899, stated at the end of an extensive report on the conditions on the island: "During the last year every officer on this Island has been overtaxed with work, and from their constant intermingling with civil affairs, they have almost lost their identity as military persons, and their military duties have greatly suffered in consequence. Of course, I realize that the officers can, and will do this work probably better than civilians, but there is a limit even to an Army Officer's endurance" (Aguadilla Letters Sent, vol. 2, no. 305, p. 46).

66. Good examples of this spirit were Captain Macomb, the commander in Arecibo, and Lieutenant Chiles, the commander in Aguadilla. The latter wrote on September 20, 1899, to the adjutant general of the department: "whether it is possible ever to instill true American instincts and truly Americanize a people, other than Anglo-Saxon . . . remains to be seen" (Ibid., 38).

Bibliography

MANUSCRIPT SOURCES

Archivo General de Puerto Rico:
  Fondo de Gobernadores Españoles de Puerto Rico
  Fondo Diputación Provincial
  Fondo de Obras Públicas
  Fondo de la Fortaleza
  Fondo de Justicia, Serie Confinados
  Fondo Municipal de Utuado
  Fondo Tribunal Superior de Arecibo
  Fondo Tribunal Superior de Ponce

Archivo Municipal de Ponce
Archivo de la Parroquia San Miguel de Utuado
National Archives and Records Administration, Washington, D.C.:
  Record Group 108
  Record Group 153
  Record Group 395

PRINTED SOURCES

Ashford, Bailey K. *A Soldier in Science: The Autobiography of Bailey K. Ashford.* New York: William Morrow, 1934.

Bartholomew, Charles Lewis. *Cartoons of the Spanish-American War with Dates of Important Events.* Minneapolis: Journal Printing Co., 1899.

Bothwell González, Reece B. *Puerto Rico: Cien años de lucha política.* Río Piedras: University of Puerto Rico Press, 1979.

Carroll, Henry K. *Report on the Island of Porto Rico: Its Population, Civil Government, Commerce, Industries, Production, Roads, Tariff, and Currency, with Recommendations.* Treasury Dept. Document no. 2118. Washington: U.S. Government Printing Office, 1899.

Coll y Toste, Cayetano. *Reseña del estado social, económico e industrial de la isla de Puerto Rico al tomar posesión de ella los Estados Unidos.* San Juan: La Correspondencia Press, 1899.

Davis, Richard Harding. *The Cuban and Porto Rican Campaigns.* New York: Scribner's, 1898.

———. *Notes of a War Correspondent.* New York: Scribner's, 1911.

Edwards, Frank E. *The '98 Campaign of the 6th Massachusetts. U.S.V.* Boston: n.p., 1899.

Fiala, Anthony. *Troop "C" in Service: An Account of the Part Played by Troop "C" of the New York Volunteer Cavalry in the Spanish American War of 1898.* New York: Eagle, 1899.

Herrmann, Karl Stephen. *From Yauco to Las Marías. Being a Story of the Recent Campaign in Western Puerto Rico by the Independent Regular Brigade, under Command of Brigadier-General Schwan.* Boston: R. G. Badger, 1900.

Keenan, Henry F. *The Conflict with Spain: A History of the War: Based Upon Official Reports and Descriptions of Eye Witnesses.* Philadelphia and Chicago: F.W. Ziegler, 1898.

Lee, Albert E. *An Island Grows: Memoirs of Albert E. Lee, Puerto Rico 1873–1942.* San Juan: A.E. Lee & Son, 1963.

Martínez Mirabal, Julio Tomás. *Colección Martínez: Crónicas íntimas.* Arecibo: n.p., 1946.

Miles, Nelson A. *Serving the Republic: Memoirs of the Civil and Military Life of Nelson A. Miles, Lieutenant General, United States Army.* New York: Harper & Bros., 1911.

Nieves, Juan B. *La anexión de Puerto Rico a los Estados Unidos de América.* Ponce, 1898.

Olivares, José de. *Our Islands and Their People as Seen with Camera and*

Pencil. Edited and arranged by William S. Bryan. St. Louis, New York, etc.: N.D. Thompson, 1899.

Picó, Fernando, ed. "Informe del General Ulysses S. Grant, hijo, al Ayudante General del Departamento de Puerto Rico sobre las Condiciones Sociales y Económicas de Puerto Rico, en marzo 1899," *Historia y Sociedad* X (1998): 129–34.

———. "Informe del Teniente Seaborn G. Chiles, del 11mo. de Infantería, al Ayudante General de Puerto Rico sobre las Condiciones Sociales y Económicas de Puerto Rico, en marzo, 1899," *Historia y Sociedad* 10 (1998): 135–44.

Sandburg, Carl. *Always the Young Strangers.* New York: Harcourt, 1953.

Seager, Robert II, and Doris D. Maguire, eds. *Letters and Papers of Alfred Thayer Mahan. Vol. 11: 1890–1901.* Annapolis: Naval Inst. Press, 1975.

Torre, Jovino de Ia. *Siluetas Ponceñas: Estudios analíticos de los principales personajes de Ia Ciudad de Ponce.* Ponce: Imprenta J. Picó Matos, 1900.

United States. Congress. House. *Official Army Register 1897.* 54th Cong. 2nd Session. Doc. no. 149. Washington, 1896.

United States. Congress. *Papers Relating to the Foreign Relations of the United States with the Annual Message of the President Transmitted to Congress December 5, 1898.* Washington, 1899.

Van Dusen, Lewis Harlow, et al. *Quinquennial Records of the Class of 'Ninety-Eight of Princeton University.* Philadelphia: n.p., 1903.

NEWSPAPERS

A. *Puerto Rican Newspapers* (issues available in the Colección Puertorriqueña of the José M. Lázaro Library, University of Puerto Rico, Río Piedras Campus; in the Colección Junghanns of the Archivo General de Puerto Rico; and in the Colección Puertorriqueña in the Sacred Heart University of Puerto Rico).

El Boletín Mercantil
La Bomba (first series: 1895; second series: 1800)
La Bruja
El Combate
El Correo de Puerto Rico
La Correspondencia de Puerto Rico
La Democracia
La Estrella Solitaria
La Federación Obrera
Frégoli
La Gaceta del Gobierno de Puerto Rico
La Metralla
El País
The San Juan News
El Territorio
La Unión
El Vesuvius

B. *American Newspapers*
(microfilms in the Library of Northwestern University)

Chicago Daily News
Chicago Tribune
New York Herald
New York Times
New York Tribune

FOR FURTHER REFERENCE

'98 Cien Años Después. Ponce: Museo de Arte de Ponce, 1999.
Albizu-Campos, Pedro. *Obras Escogidas*, Benjamín Torres, ed. San Juan, 1981.
Alvarez Curbelo, Silvia, Mary Frances Gallart, and Carmen I. Raffucci, eds. *Los arcos de la memoria: El '98 de los pueblos puertorriqueños.*

San Juan: Asociación Puertorriqueña de Historiadores, 1998.

Barbosa de Rosario, Pilar. *El ensayo de la autonomía en Puerto Rico 1897–1898*. San Juan: n.p., 1975. Vol. 7 of *La Obra de José Celso Barbosa*.

Barceló Miller, María. *Política ultramarina y gobierno municipal: Isabela, 1873–1887*. Río Piedras: Huracán, 1984.

Beisner, Robert L. *Twelve Against Empire: The Anti-imperialists, 1898–1900*. New York: n.p., 1968.

Berbusse, Edward J., S.J. *The United States in Puerto Rico 1898–1900*. Chapel Hill: University of North Carolina Press, 1966.

Bergad, Laird W. *Coffee and the Growth of Agrarian Capitalism in Nineteenth-Century Puerto Rico*. Princeton: Princeton University Press, 1983.

Bonnin Orozco, María Isabel. "Las fortunas vulnerables: comerciantes y agricultores en los contratos de refacción de Ponce, 1865–1875." MA Thesis, University of Puerto Rico, Río Piedras, 1984.

Bowers, Claude G. *Beveridge and the Progressive Era*. Cambridge, Mass.: Houghton, 1932.

Brown, Charles H. *The Correspondents' War: Journalists in the Spanish-American War*. New York: Scribner's, 1967.

Buitrago Ortiz, Carlos. *Haciendas cafetaleras y clases terratenientes en el Puerto Rico decimonónico*. Río Piedras: University of Puerto Rico Press, 1982.

———. *Los orígenes históricos de la sociedad precapitalista en Puerto Rico (ensayos de etnohistoria puertorriqueña)*. Río Piedras: Huracán, 1976.

Burgos Malavé, Eda M., ed. *El conflicto de 1898: Antecedentes y Consecuencias Inmediatas*. Río Piedras: Universidad de Puerto Rico, 2000.

Cabranes, José A. *Citizenship and the American Empire: Notes on the Legislative History of the United States Citizenship of Puerto Ricans*. New Haven: Yale University Press, 1979.

Casanova, Carlos. "Propiedad agrícola y poder en el municipio de Manatí: 1885–1898." MA Thesis, University of Puerto Rico, Río Piedras, 1985.

Cifre de Loubriel, EsteIa. *La formación del pueblo puertorriqueño: La contribución de los catalanes, baleáricos y valencianos.* San Juan: Inst. de Cultura Puertorriqueña, 1975.

Córdova Chirino, Jacobo. *Los que murieron en la horca: Historia del crimen, juicio y ajusticiamientos de los que en Puerto Rico murieron en la horca desde las Partidas Sediciosas (1898) a Pascual Ramos (15 de septiembre de 1927).* San Juan: Cordillera, 1975.

Cruz Monclova, Lidio. *Historia del año de 1887.* Río Piedras: University of Puerto Rico Press, 1970.

―――. *Historia de Puerto Rico (siglo XIX).* 6th ed. Río Piedras: University of Puerto Rico Press, 1970.

Cubano Iguina, Astrid Teresa. "Comercio y hegemonía social: Los comerciantes de Arecibo, 1857–1887." MA Thesis, University of Puerto Rico, Río Piedras, 1979.

Dávila Santiago, Rubén. "El derribo de las murallas y el porvenir de Borinquen." *Cuadernos CEREP, Serie investigación y análisis* 8 (1983): n.p.

Delgado, Juan Manuel. *El levantamiento de Ciales.* Río Piedras: Guasábara, 1980.

Delgado Pasapera, Germán. *Puerto Rico: Sus luchas emancipadoras (1850–1898).* Río Piedras: Cultural, 1984.

Díaz Hernández, Luis Edgardo. *Castañer: Una hacienda cafetalera en Puerto Rico (1868–1930).* 2nd ed. Río Piedras: Edil, 1983.

Díaz Soler, Luis M. *Rosendo Matienzo Cintrón: Orientador y guardián de una cultura.* Río Piedras: Inst. de Lit. Puertorriqueña, UPR, 1960.

Ferreras Pagán, J. *Biografía de las riquezas de Puerto Rico.* San Juan: L. Ferreras, 1902.

Figueroa, Loida. *Breve historia de Puerto Rico.* Segunda parte: Desde el crepúsculo del dominio español hasta la antesala de la Ley Foraker 1892–1900. Río Piedras: Edil, 1977.

Foner, Philip S. *The Spanish-Cuban-American War and the Birth of American Imperialism.* New York: Monterey Review, 1972.

Freire, Joaquín. *Presencia de Puerto Rico en la historia de Cuba (Una aportación al estudio de la historia antillana).* San Juan: Inst. de

Cultura Puertorriqueña, 1975.

García, Gervasio L., and A.G. Quintero Rivera. *Desafío y solidaridad: Breve historia del movimiento obrero puertorriqueño.* Río Piedras: Huracán, 1982.

García Ochoa, María Asunción. *La política española en Puerto Rico durante el siglo XIX.* Río Piedras: University of Puerto Rico Press, 1982.

García Rodríguez, Gervasio L. *Historia crítica, historia sin coartadas: Algunos problemas de la historia de Puerto Rico.* Río Piedras: Huracán, 1985.

———. "Primeros fermentos de organización obrera en Puerto Rico 1873–1898." *Cuadernos CEREP* I (1974): n.p.

Gautier Dapena, José A. *Trayectoria del pensamiento liberal puertorriqueño en el siglo XIX.* San Juan: Inst. de Cultura Puertorriqueña, 1963.

Gaztambide-Géigel, Antonio, Juan González-Mendoza, and Mario R. Cancel. *Cien años de sociedad: Los 98 del Gran Caribe.* San Juan: Asociación Puertorriqueña de Historiadores and Ediciones Callejón, 2000.

Gil de Rubio, Víctor M. *Periodismo patriótico de Evaristo Izcoa Díaz (Biografía).* San Juan: Liga de Coop. de Puerto Rico, 1977.

Girón, Socorro. *Ponce, el Teatro La Perla y "La Campana de la Almudaina."* Ponce: S. Girón, 1986.

González, Lydia Milagros, and Ángel G. Quintero Rivera. *La otra cara de la historia: la historia de Puerto Rico desde su cara obrera. Vol. 1: 1800–1925.* Río Piedras: CEREP, 1984.

González Vales, Luis E., ed. *1898: Enfoques y perspectivas: Simposio internacional de historiadores.* San Juan: Academia Puertorriqueña de Historiadores, 1997.

Gould, Lyman J. *La Ley Foraker: Raíces de la política colonial de los Estados Unidos.* Translated by Jorge Luis Morales. Río Piedras: University of Puerto Rico Press, 1969. Originally *The Foraker Act: The Roots of American Colonial Policy.* Ann Arbor, Mich.: University Microfilms, 1958.

Hall, A.D. *Cuba: Its Past, Present, and Future; Porto Rico: Its History, Products and Possibilities.* New York: Street & Smith, 1898.

Hays, Samuel P. *The Response to Industrialism, 1885–1914.* The Chicago History of American Civilization. Chicago: University of Chicago Press, 1957 (8th printing, 1964).

Hill, Robert T. *Cuba and Porto Rico With the Other Islands of the West Indies: Their Topography, Climate, Flora, Products, Industries, Cities, People, Political Conditions, Etc.* 2nd ed. New York: The Century, 1899.

Hobsbawm, Eric J. *Primitive Rebels: Studies in Archaic Forms of Social Movements in the 19th and 20th Centuries.* Manchester: Manchester University Press, 1959.

Iglesias Pantín, Santiago. *Luchas emancipadoras: Crónicas de Puerto Rico.* 2nd ed. San Juan: n.p., 1958.

Jessup, Philip C. *Elihu Root.* 3rd printing. New York: Dodd, 1938.

Kaplan, Temma. *Anarchists of Andalusia, 1868–1903.* Princeton: Princeton University Press, 1977.

Katsilis Morales, Peter. "Economía y sociedad del pueblo de Camuy, 1850–1868." MA Thesis, University of Puerto Rico, Río Piedras, 1986.

Luque de Sánchez, María Dolores. *La ocupación norteamericana y la Ley Foraker (La opinión pública puertorriqueña).* Río Piedras: University of Puerto Rico Press, 1980.

Mayol, Esperanza. *Islas: Autobiografía.* Palma de Mallorca: n.p., 1974.

Naranjo, Consuelo, Miguel A. Puig Samper, and Luis Miguel García Mora. *La Nación Soñada: Cuba, Puerto Rico y Filipinas ante el 98.* Madrid: Editorial Doce Calles, 1996.

Naranjo Orovio, Consuelo, and Carlos Serrano, eds. *Imágenes e imaginarios nacionales en el Ultramar español.* Madrid: Casa de Velásquez, 1999.

Negrón Portillo, Mariano. *Cuadrillas anexionistas y revueltas campesinas en Puerto Rico, 1898–1899.* Río Piedras: Centro de Investigaciones Sociales, 1987.

———. *El autonomismo puertorriqueño: su transformación ideológica (1895–1914): La prensa en el análisis social: La Democracia de*

Puerto Rico. Río Piedras: Huracán, 1981.

———. "El liderato anexionista antes y después del cambio de soberanía." *Revista del Colegio de Abogados* 33 (1972): 369–91.

Offner, John L. *An Unwanted War: The Diplomacy of the United States and Spain over Cuba, 1895–1898.* Chapel Hill: The University of North Carolina Press, 1992.

Ortiz Cuadra, Cruz. "Crédito y azúcar: Los hacendados de Humacao ante la crisis del dulce: 1865–1900." MA Thesis, University of Puerto Rico, Río Piedras, 1985.

O'Toole, G.J.A. *The Spanish War: An American Epic 1898.* New York: Norton, 1984.

Pérez, Louis A. *Army Politics in Cuba, 1898–1958.* Pittsburgh: University of Pittsburgh Press, 1976.

———. "Insurrection, Intervention and the Transformation of Land Tenure Systems in Cuba, 1895–1902." *The Hispanic American Historical Review* 65 (1985): 229–54.

Picó, Fernando. *Cada Guaraguao: Galería de Oficiales Norteamericanos en Puerto Rico.* Río Piedras: Ediciones Huracán, 1998.

———. *Contra la Corriente: Seis Microbiografías de Tiempos de España.* Río Piedras: Ediciones Huracán, 1996.

———. *Historia General de Puerto Rico.* Río Piedras: Ediciones Huracán, 1986.

———. "La revolución puertorriqueña de 1898: La necesidad de un nuevo paradigma para entender el 1898 puertorriqueño." *Historia y Sociedad* 10 (1998): 7–22.

Poumier-Taquechel, Maria. *Contribution à l'étude du banditisme social à Cuba: L'histoire et le mythe de Manuel García "Rey de los Campos de Cuba" (1851–1895).* Lille: n.p., 1986.

Quintero Rivera, Ángel G. *Conflictos de clase y política en Puerto Rico.* Río Piedras: Huracán, 1976.

Raffucci, Carmen I. *El gobierno civil y la Ley Foraker.* Río Piedras: University of Puerto Rico Press, 1981.

Ramos Mattei, Andrés. *La hacienda azucarera: Su crecimiento y crisis en Puerto Rico (siglo XIX).* San Juan: CEREP, 1981.

Rickover, H.G. *How the Battleship Maine Was Destroyed.* Washington, D.C.: GPO, 1976.

Rivero, Ángel. *Crónica de la Guerra Hispanoamericana en Puerto Rico.* San Juan: Edil, 1972.

Rodríguez, Paulino. *Historia del pueblo de Patillas.* Hato Rey: n.p., 1968.

Rodríguez Díaz, María del Rosario, ed. *1898: Entre la continuidad y la ruptura.* Morelia: Universidad Michoacana de San Nicolás de Hidalgo, 1997.

Rosa Martínez, Luis de la. *Léxicon histórico-documental de Puerto Rico (1812–1899).* San Juan: Centro de Estudios Avanzados de Puerto Rico y el Caribe, 1986.

Rosado Ruiz, Carlos. "Grupos dominantes: Hacendados y comerciantes en el antiguo partido de Utuado, 1850–1868." MA Thesis, University of Puerto Rico, Río Piedras, 1986.

Rosario Natal, Carmelo. *El 1898 puertorriqueño en la historiografía: Ensayo y bibliografía crítica.* San Juan: Academia Puertorriqueña de la Historia, 1997.

———. *Puerto Rico y la crisis de la Guerra Hispanoamericana (1895–1898).* Hato Rey: Edil, 1975.

Santiago de Curet, Ana Mercedes. "Crédito, moneda y bancos en Puerto Rico durante el siglo XIX." MA Thesis, University of Puerto Rico, Río Piedras, 1978.

Scarano, Francisco A. *Sugar and Slavery in Puerto Rico: The Plantation Economy of Ponce. 1800–1850.* Madison: University of Wisconsin Press, 1984.

Seager, Robert II. *Alfred Thayer Mahan: The Man and His Letters.* Annapolis: Naval Inst. Press, 1977.

Serrano, Carlos. *Final del Imperio. España 1895–1898.* Madrid: n.p., 1984.

Silvestrini, Blanca G., ed. *Politics, Society and Culture in the Caribbean: Selected Papers of the XIV Conference of Caribbean Historians.* San Juan: University of Puerto Rico, 1983.

———. *Violencia y criminalidad en Puerto Rico 1898–1973: Apuntes para un estudio de historia social.* Río Piedras: University of Puerto

Rico Press, 1980.

Smith, Angel, and Emma Dávila-Cox. *The Crisis of 1898: Colonial Redistribution and Nationalist Mobilization.* New York: St. Martin's Press, 1999.

Thompson, Lanny. *Nuestra isla y su gente: La construcción del "otro" puertorriqueño en Our Islands and Their People.* Río Piedras: Centro de Investigaciones Sociales, 1995.

Tirado Merced, Dulce María. "Las raíces sociales del liberalismo criollo: El Partido Liberal Reformista (1870–1875)." MA Thesis, University of Puerto Rico, Río Piedras, 1981.

Tolman, Newton F. *The Search for General Miles.* New York: Putnam, 1968.

Trías Monge, José. *Historia constitucional de Puerto Rico.* Río Piedras: University of Puerto Rico Press, 1980–83.

Vales, Pedro A., Astrid A. Ortiz, and Noel F. Mattei. *Patrones de criminalidad en Puerto Rico: Apreciación socio-histórica: 1898–1980.* Río Piedras: n.p., 1982.